ARE YOU READY TO SUCCEED?

———◆———

ARE YOU READY TO SUCCEED?

UNCONVENTIONAL STRATEGIES FOR ACHIEVING
PERSONAL MASTERY IN BUSINESS AND LIFE

SRIKUMAR S. RAO

New York

Grateful acknowledgment is made for permission to include mate-rial from THE WAY TO LOVE: THE LAST MEDITATIONS OF A. DE MELLO by J. Francis Stroud, copyright © 1991 by Gujarat Sahitya Prakash of Anand, India. Introduction copyright © 1992 by J. Francis Stroud. Used by permission of Doubleday, a division of Random House, Inc.

Library of Congress Cataloging-in-Publication Data

Rao, Srikumar S.
    Are you ready to succeed? : unconventional strategies for
  achieving personal mastery in business and life / Srikumar S. Rao.
      p. cm.
  Includes bibliographical references.
  ISBN 1-4013-0193-2
    1. Success—Psychological aspects. 2. Success in business—
  Psychological aspects. 3. Self-actualization (Psychology) I. Title.

  BF637.S8R28 2006
  158.1—dc22   2005052559

Hyperion books are available for special promotions and premiums. For details contact Michael Rentas, Assistant Director, Inventory Operations, Hyperion, 77 West 66th Street, 11th floor, New York, New York 10023, or call 212-456-0133.

FIRST EDITION

10 9 8 7 6 5 4 3

Dedicated to:
Bhagvan Ramana Maharshi

H. H. Jagadguru Sri Abhinava Vidyatirtha Mahaswamigal, the 35th
Shankaracharya of Sri Sarada Peetham, Sringeri

And
My mother
and the tradition they belonged to.

And also to:
My wife, Meena, who bore a disproportionate share of the
burden of running a house while I developed the course and did
the actual writing.

My daughter, Gowri, who unfailingly cheered me on
when I was flagging.

My son, Gautam, who discovered one of his passions while still in
school—I wish I had found it so early!

CONTENTS

CONTENTS

ARE YOU READY TO SUCCEED?

———◆———

An Exhilarating Journey— the Beginning

———✦———

What if I were to tell you that you live in a dreamworld and that you have always been living in a dreamworld. That you have never known anything but this dreamworld. What if I were to go on and explain that you, who have spent your whole life so carefully constructing this world, have put a great deal of stuff in it that you don't really like—things that cause you to moan and groan, sometimes very loudly indeed. Things that frequently make you miserable, and others as well. If you are like most people, you will think, "Nonsense. This is no fantasy, it's my life." I understand that it's hard to accept that your reality is but a shadow, and one that you created. Instead, it's easier to dismiss what I say and persist in thinking that what you recognize as your life is "real" and that it somehow simply "happened." You had nothing—or very little—to do with it. And THAT, I am here to tell you, is the source, the root cause of ALL of your problems.

Knowing that you are living in a dreamworld is actually very liberating, because it gives you the option of waking up. I sincerely hope that you are ready to do so. If you are not yet ready to do so, you have another option—you can at least create a new, better dreamworld.

This book will show you how. And, regardless of whether you wake up or create a better dreamworld, you will find that life has become richer. The colors you see are more vibrant, your interactions with others are more fulfilling, and you experience more joyous moments. You become more effective at work and enjoy it more.

I know this is so, because it happened to me and because I have helped hundreds of others get there.

Three decades ago, I was a doctoral student in marketing at the Graduate School of Business, Columbia University. Initially, I was thrilled to be in a top business school in one of the great universities of the world, but as time went on I found myself profoundly unsettled by what I saw around me. I read academic papers and doctoral dissertations with sentences like, "Item structure congruence methods aim to address the issue of operationalization equivalence. They presuppose construct equivalence and confine their testing to components of the construct. . . ." Increasingly, I was filled with wonderment—a wonderment that expressed itself as, "For this, they killed a tree?" So much of academic "research" seemed so utterly bereft of any redeeming or lasting value that I could not fathom how bright, even brilliant, people could be so wrapped up in it.

I tried desperately to find meaning in my own research, to pump up my enthusiasm and sagging motivation. I failed. Ultimately, sheer force of will enabled me to complete my doctorate. Sadly, the joy I felt on receiving my diploma didn't come from a sense of accomplishment but from the knowledge that my painful graduate days were finally over.

I entered the workforce. In very little time, I could have sworn that the world consisted of two sets of people: those who passionately loathed their jobs and those who simply disliked them. As for me, I busily alternated between the two. It wasn't fun, but I didn't know that anything else existed. The notion that one could find deep meaning and sustenance from life and from what one did for a living was an alien one.

Searching to quell my dissatisfaction, after a few years I left private enterprise and took a position in academe. Simultaneously I started writing and eventually became a contributing editor for *Financial World* and, later, *Forbes.* It gradually dawned on me that I was hardly alone in my unhappiness. As I spoke to thousands of undergraduates, graduate students, doctoral candidates, and corporate managers, I saw that most could readily identify with my feelings of angst and ennui, and many had tales of their own.

I knew there had to be a better way. Life was not meant to be like this. If I felt trapped, then so must thousands of others with whom I had spoken and, by extension, millions of others in the broader world. I was so busy wallowing in my own misery I barely noticed that there were some free spirits who had escaped my fate and who soared effortlessly over the quicksand that kept sucking me in. It was not until much later that I realized they were the real teachers and the ones worth emulating.

During this period, the one truly bright spot in my life was reading. I had been a voracious reader all my life, particularly philosophy, spiritual biography, and mystical autobiography from many different times and traditions. The stories and their wisdom gave me my only sense of hope that there was something powerful, meaningful, and good at work in the universe. Immersed in these books I would feel the peace and the ineffable sense of well-being I sought. But the mundane demands of the world would inevitably come creeping back, and they were wonderfully effective at suffocating the freedom I experienced during such reading.

I felt like the water buffaloes that, during hot summer days in tropical countries, like to wallow in the muddy water. After all, it keeps them cool and comfortable. But there are flies and mosquitoes and other biting insects with mandibles and proboscides strong enough to penetrate even their thick skin. They cover the backs of the buffaloes like a blanket. When the pain gets too intense, the buffalo dives into the water and experiences blessed relief. The insects rise off its back in a swarm. But they hover in the air. They know the buffalo will surface soon, and the moment it does, they will descend and continue their feeding.

It was a perfect visual metaphor for the way I felt. The insects— the gnawing insecurities, worries, anxieties, jealousies, irritations, concerns, fears, guilt, and apprehensions—kept coming back. And each time they returned, they seemed stronger and more fearsome.

Gradually I realized that my life need not be like this. My mental insects could be banished, and relatively easily. I could submerge like the buffalo, but I did not have to surface at the same spot. I could swim a hundred feet underwater and emerge in a spot clear of pests. The pests will come back, but the process can easily be repeated. Freedom IS possible.

I began to think about the toll this pestilence was taking on the students. After all, these were men and women destined to be leaders in business. To a person, each thrived on challenge, pursued accomplishment, dreamed of success, and sought a position of responsibility and leadership. But how, I wondered, could these students hope to inspire others or accomplish their ambitions when they, themselves, felt devoured by their own lives?

It was clear to me that students were focusing on the wrong things. They were far too fixated on money, power, and prestige.

They evaluated opportunities based on what they could get out of them. Many were prepared to make incredible sacrifices, to work hellish hours, in order to "make it," but the price they paid was far too high. I knew I could help them achieve even better results with far less anguish by teaching them a series of simple switches in the way they approached life, such as by focusing on what they could contribute rather than what they could get. This one simple switch in attention could, by itself, help propel them to undreamed-of success. I had many such tools, but the problem was getting the students to truly understand their power.

I devised a course to help these students achieve a breakthrough in their lives, one that would enable them to be true leaders. On the surface, the syllabus had nothing to do with traditional business principles and so I was unsure if anyone would be interested in something that wouldn't immediately lead to a business specialty. After all, most of the students I encountered were so goal directed that they were like the young man in the parable:

A desperate young seeker banged on the door of the Master. "I want to be enlightened," he gasped when the Master answered. "If I stay as your disciple, how long will it take?"

The Master surveyed the young man. He had a strong physique, and the inner restlessness that drove him was almost palpable. A good candidate. "Ten years," said the Master.

The youth wilted, as if struck with an ax. For a few minutes he stood with head bowed, then he looked up. "If I work night and day," he asked fiercely, "if I do without sleep and do twice what your other disciples do, then how long will it take for me to become enlightened?"

"Twenty years," said the Master calmly. So perplexed was the youth and so earnest his demeanor that the sage relented and explained,

"When you have one eye so firmly fixed on the goal, you have but one eye left to find the way."

I firmly believed that until the students found their way, they would never be able to live powerful lives—personally or professionally. I created the course that became Creativity and Personal Mastery and offered it for the first time in the fall of 1994 at Long Island University. It did well. I modified it and offered it again. It did better. I moved it to Columbia Business School. After two years, it caught fire. There were phalanxes of applicants from business school, from law school, from the School of International and Public Affairs, from journalism school, and from other divisions. The application process was cumbersome and exacting, but the call was so powerful that those who heard it jumped readily through the hoops I set up.

Over the years, people of all ages and stages of life have heard the call. Senior executives and entrepreneurs signed up for programs I ran. Alumni told friends, siblings, significant others, relatives, business acquaintances, and others, and news of the offering spread by word of mouth.

From the very beginning, I envisaged all those associated with the course—the students, guest speakers, teaching assistants, etc.— as a community. Drawing loosely from the Buddhist notion of "sangha" (a group of practitioners who travel the path together), I intended it to be a source of ongoing support and inspiration. This worked. To my knowledge, it is still the only course at any top business school that has its own alumni association. The bonds formed are deep and frequently span generations. The course was designed not to have an "end." Students embarked on a journey of exploration and growth that was expected to last decades, even a lifetime.

Here are some of the transformative experiences reported: depression being replaced with deep-seated optimism and joy; warm relations developing with an estranged parent; changes in career path in line with innate interest and passion; an astonishing turnabout in job-interviewing skills—rejection changing to nearly 100 percent callbacks; unbelievable, almost miraculous, "coincidences," from tough professors easily agreeing to changes in dissertation topics to uncompromising employers okaying flexible job arrangements; a profound reconnection with spirituality and a newfound ability to infuse it into all aspects of life with no inherent contradiction; an extraordinary increase in effectiveness—three to four times as much accomplished with less strain and effort; clarity about personal values and how to shape jobs, relationships, and other activities so they are in conformity with each other.

Quite a few "graduates" have reported that the changes have affected every part of their lives. Numerous significant others have said "Thank you" as they observed noteworthy positive changes in their partners.

I still teach the course. But the time has now come to write down the principles so that anyone who applies the tools can be transformed and can live a life of creativity and personal mastery. This book is an outgrowth of the course and also contains new exercises and fresh material. But it is not a traditional book. It is designed to produce fundamental change in your life. The book is the catalyst and the tool chest, but YOU will produce that change. Only you can produce such change.

Why This Book Can Make Miracles Happen

It would be supremely egotistical for me to proclaim that "my ideas" can produce such changes in people's lives. But I can confidently make such a claim because none of the viewpoints, exercises, and assignments I am putting down is my own. They have been articulated, tested, and refined by persons of vast wisdom and spiritual accomplishment, true giants who strode this earth. They lived at different times, belonged to different traditions, and had a deep understanding and compassion for human predicaments. Having themselves transcended these dilemmas, they devised effective methods to help their followers do the same. If you feel any power in this book, it comes from them. All I have done is to put their teachings in a cloak acceptable to educated people in a postindustrial society.

The fortress was under attack. A tall siege tower had been constructed on a nearby prominence and archers were raining down arrows and flaming missiles. Conditions were desperate.

The defending general was competent and crafty. He bided his time while the invaders built the tower, using up scarce wood and metal. In the darkness of night, he unleashed his riposte.

The royal elephant was covered with specially designed armor, and its keeper rode it to the tower before jabbing it with his ankus and leaping off onto the branch of a nearby tree, then clambering to safety.

The elephant rammed the siege tower with full force. Wood splintered and broke, supporting beams collapsed, archers tumbled from their perches and were trod, the fire basin fell on its side and flames soon consumed the structure.

The elephant strode majestically on. A flea, lodged in the elephant's ear, looked back at the destruction and chortled, "We certainly shook them up!"

I am like that flea, except that I know the elephant is doing all the work. The teachings are the elephant, and it is the elephant that will destroy the demons besieging you.

Your life is a creation. It is a work of art no less than the paintings on the ceiling of the Sistine Chapel or the giant statue of Gomateshwara at Sravanabelagola. You are the artist. *All works of art first come into being in the mind of the craftsman.* This book is an invitation to you to explore and define what you want to create.

Read this book with the expectation that it will change your life. Profoundly change your life. Utterly transform it in myriad large and small ways. Expect it to have an impact on your career, your relationships, your health, your financial well-being, your spiritual development, and every other part of your existence. It can do this. The workshop on which it is based has done it for many already. The only question is—are YOU ready?

More than a hundred years ago, an advertisement for Lydia Pinkham's Vegetable Compound made the following modest claims:

> It will cure entirely the worst form of Female Complaints, all Ovarian troubles, Inflammation and Ulceration, Falling and Displacements, and the consequent Spinal Weakness, and is particularly adapted to the Change of Life.
>
> It will dissolve and expel tumors from the uterus in an early stage of development.
>
> It removes faintness, flatulency, destroys all craving for stimulants and relieves weakness of the stomach. It cures Bloating, Headaches, Nervous Prostration, General Debility, Sleeplessness, Depression and Indigestion.
>
> That feeling of bearing down, causing pain, weight, and backache is always permanently cured by its use.
>
> For the cure of Kidney complaints of either sex, this Compound is unsurpassed.

On the off chance that the reader still does not grasp the virtues of this remarkable product, the advertisement throws in another explicit guarantee: It turns out that Lydia Pinkham's Vegetable Compound also cures cancer.

If you feel that in this book you have stumbled on a latter-day version of this miracle item, I don't blame you. It sure sounds like it. Bear with me while I explain in greater detail what this book can do and why it can indeed do this. Then examine yourself carefully to see if you are willing to put the principles into practice. If you honestly are, then you will assuredly find that it delivers on its promise.

HOW TO USE THIS BOOK

If you dip in and out of this book, only occasionally practicing the exercises, you will undoubtedly derive some benefit, but it is unlikely that your life will be transformed. In my experience, the major difference that separates those who receive remarkable results from those who enjoy only modest improvements is that the latter find innumerable and ingenious ways not to do the recommended assignments and exercises. There are so many plausible, even urgent, reasons to let life encroach and to not do the hard, introspective self-examination necessary. But the motivated reader finds a way to make the time to do the work. The partially engaged reader does not.

This all might sound very strenuous and arduous. It's not. Think of it this way: If you have dry gunpowder in an oxygen-rich atmosphere and you bring in a lighted match, the explosion will happen. You don't have to expend a lot of energy. No heroic effort is needed. You just need to let the match touch the powder. The ideas and exercises in this book are the match. You are the gunpowder, and the oxygen is everywhere. Your part in the process is to be open-minded and willing. This means that you conscientiously and sincerely do the exercises. And repeat them if necessary.

There are assignments and exercises throughout this book. It is important that you:

1. **Do the exercises in the order in which they are presented.**
   Some of the learning is subtle and you may not even realize what you have learned till long afterward. Also, later assignments build on earlier ones, so skipping around is counterproductive. The steeple goes on the church AFTER the foundation is laid and the main floors are constructed!

2. **Really, really, really give the exercises your very best shot.**
   Invest yourself in them emotionally and psychically. The biggest payoff comes when you succeed in this.

   Have you ever seen an amateur play, such as one produced by your high school or the local library? There are many characters who walk woodenly across the stage and are clearly uncomfortable mouthing their lines. And there are always some who "get into" their roles with vim and vigor. And as they do, they also connect with the audience. They are the ones who get the applause and truly enjoy the fun of the experience. You want to be the latter.

   There will be times when you feel that you are going through the motions. When you "do" an exercise but it feels mechanical and contrived. When you receive no insights and, worse, actually feel annoyed and resentful.

If this happens, take a break. Sometimes a day or two is sufficient. Sometimes you may need a week or more. But come back to it. Keep coming back until you have done the exercise with the enthusiasm of the actor who gets into the assigned role. It is only after you have done this that you can decide whether or not the exercise worked for you.

Many of the exercises are really elaborate thought experiments. You have to learn how to make them work. The good news is that this is a skill and can be mastered with practice. The bad news is that you need steady persistence. Without this ability to stick at it, you will give up too soon and all you will have gained is one more book gathering dust on your shelves.

3. **Create a support group.**

    It is an excellent idea to put together a group of three to six people—perhaps friends and associates—who are all working with the book at approximately the same speed. Meet regularly—once every two weeks if you can. Compare notes and insights. Ask the questions that arise— just the articulation of these frequently brings clarity.

    Not only will this be pleasant company, it will also be a powerful support network.

4. **Begin keeping a journal.**

    Start today. It's okay to keep it on your laptop if you really want to, but I recommend an old-fashioned diary with bound pages in which you write in longhand— there is something magical and binding about the act of writing.

Make an entry every day; more than one entry a day also works. Record whatever strikes you as you read the book and do the exercises. Particularly note any insights that you discover. How do they affect your life? Do you see that they can have an even more powerful effect?

5. **Note your emotional tenor on a day-by-day basis.**
   Explicitly state this in your journal. How was it before you started the book and how is it changing? Make a note of what you intend to follow up on. Then do it!

Mental Model for Reading This Book

In this book, I will talk a lot about mental models. A "mental model" is a notion we have of how the world works, of how things ought to be done or are done. We use mental models to explain to our satisfaction why things happen. We use them to console ourselves and to tell us what we should do. Most of the time—and this is the real killer—we don't even recognize that we are using mental models.

Although I will go into this subject in greater depth in the next chapter, it's important to offer the mental model I recommend using as you read this book:

1. The author says this book can dramatically change my life. I will be open to this because I *want* this change in my life.

2. I will read this book carefully, using my highlighter to mark passages that strike me. Every time I come across an idea that really excites me, I will stop reading.

3. I will ponder that idea and explore its ramifications. I will keep bringing it to mind at odd moments until I feel completely comfortable with it.

4. I will start a journal as recommended and make entries regularly and frequently.

5. I will practice the exercises in the order presented. I will invest considerable emotional and psychic energy in each exercise. I will carefully observe my reactions, the reactions of others with whom I am interacting, and any results and note them in my journal.

6. I will be particularly aware of my emotional state— despondent or happy? Anxious or at ease? Angry or peaceful? I will write down these states and see how they change over time as I continue to do the exercises and ponder the ideas and concepts presented.

7. I will not talk about this journey to all and sundry. I will talk about this to selected friends or relatives who are sympathetic and may have useful insights. I will encourage them to read the book as well and do the exercises so that we have more in common to discuss.

8. I recognize that this book is merely a starting point. I am launching myself onto a path of awareness and growth that will take years, decades, maybe the rest of my life. I am comfortable with this. This is what I *want*.

DO THESE EXERCISES AS IF YOU WERE WEARING A *LUNGYI* OR A SARI!

Have you ever worn a *lungyi*? Or a sari? I spent some years growing up in Burma—now Myanmar—and most men would wear *lungyis*. It's basically a piece of cloth sewn into a cylindrical tube that reaches from midriff to ankle, and men casually tie it around the waist as a lower garment. Formal ones are stiff, embroidered with metallic thread—frequently gold thread—and have intricate designs. Everyday ones can be drab or colorful but are made of inexpensive fabric. It takes seconds to put on, is very easy to launder, and provides lots of room for air to circulate. It is an eminently suitable garment for a hot, tropical country. It's easy to understand why it is part of the national dress.

It took me a long time to learn to wear a *lungyi*. If you don't tie it evenly, it wrinkles around the legs and lopsidedly shows an ankle. If you tie it too tightly, it gives you a stomachache. If you tie it too loosely, it has a tendency to slide to the floor, leaving you naked and embarrassed. You can have an expert tie it for you, but it still feels awkward and shows in the way you walk and otherwise comport yourself. It bunches up rather than flowing smoothly to the ground.

Eventually I became quite comfortable wearing a *lungyi*, but I deemed it a tremendous success if I could merely keep it on without adjusting it every few minutes. I couldn't even dream of playing *chinlon* while wearing a *lungyi*. A *chinlon* is a very light, hollow wicker ball slightly smaller than a soccer ball. Burmese, generally males, play *chinlon* all over the place. The objective is to keep the ball in play using the feet, elbows, the head, and other body parts, but not the hands. Good players twist and contort themselves as they catch it behind them, beside them, in front of them, and at all heights. They are incredibly graceful and they do it all wearing a *lungyi.*

A sari, of course, is one of the traditional dresses worn by women in India and many other countries. It is a single strip of cloth, six feet or more in length, and comes in many different textures of fabric and colors. There are numerous ways of wearing it, from demure to downright sexy, and, once again, women who wear it well look unbelievably elegant. Most Westerners who try it have to resort to hidden pins and sticky tape and are never completely at ease.

If you want to feel comfortable in a *lungyi* or a sari, there is only one way: Just wear it and keep wearing it. If you want to feel natural doing the exercises in this book, if you want to be comfortable in the world you are creating, there is only one way: Just keep doing it. As long as you look on what you are doing as an "exercise," you will feel awkward and uneasy.

If you persist, each exercise will cease being one and will become a part of you. As multiple exercises thus become an integral part of who you are, you will find that your life has changed completely and that there is no way you will ever trade in this "made-up, unreal world" for the one you had before.

If you approach the book in this spirit, all I can say is, "I salute you!" You are the reason this book came into being. Godspeed and good luck! You will be amazed by how far you will travel, and in how short a time. Your journal will reveal your progress, so keep it religiously!

CHAPTER ONE

An Ideal Life

———⊰•⊱———

*It is a beautiful spring morning. It is radiantly sunny and warm, not
hot. There is a cooling breeze and fluffy white clouds drift lazily by. A little girl skips down a path in a green, green meadow. She pauses by a fence
to pet a cow. She reaches out to catch a beautiful orange butterfly but it
flits out of reach. A rabbit, startled by her approach, drops the carrot it
was eating and scampers away. The girl laughs, the happy sounds completely filling the air with the tinkling laughter of innocence and gaiety.*

Stop right now and evaluate your life. Is it filled with that effortless
pleasure? Or drudgery? I want you to feel that effervescent joy. Ask
yourself, are there great dollops of that in your life? If not, WHY
not? Probably, many answers come to mind—work, financial obli-
gations, family responsibilities. If you are like many of the thousands of students I have taught, you probably feel somewhat
trapped—in a job you dislike, in a relationship you have outgrown,
in responsibilities that feel onerous, in surroundings that suffocate.

Do you sometimes feel like a gerbil in a wheel, or as if you were trying to run through chest-deep molasses? Do you sense that there is much that you have to do but are unsure of what, and how to go about doing whatever it is?

Go back to a time in your life when you had a deep, meaningful conversation with someone. A conversation that was rich with significance. One that nourished you on many levels. Maybe with a parent. Or a friend. Or a favorite uncle or other relative. Or with a romantic partner. Recall the feeling of closeness that you had, the affection that welled up. Remember how long it lasted and how good it felt.

When was the last time you forged such a connection with another human being? If it was more than a month ago, why? Are most—or all—of your relationships a series of meaningless interactions? This can happen with friends and colleagues. It can happen with spouses and children and parents. Is it happening with you? Do you have a series of trivial conversations on such momentous topics as where you had dinner, and what you bought, and what movie you saw or plan to see, and what some celebrity did? If you want more out of your relationships in life, in love and in work, this book will help you fashion deep connections with the people around you. Even some of your interactions with perfect strangers will become nourishing and sustaining.

Virtually everyone who has followed the program in this book reports having more deep connections with colleagues than in many previous months or years of life.

Life is short. And uncertain. It is like a drop of water skittering around on a lotus leaf. You never know when it will drop off the edge and disappear. So each day is far too precious to waste. And each day that you are not radiantly alive and brimming with cheer is a day wasted.

This book will help you stop wasting your days. It will help you discover the joy of effortless action. It will help you get started in discovering your "purpose in life," the grand design that gives meaning to all of your activities, the endeavor to which you can enthusiastically devote the rest of your life. Note that I said "get started," not "arrive at." There is a nonlinear relationship between the "work" you do and the "results" you get. Immense exertion can produce little outcome and, at other times, a little effort can yield a huge payoff. But if you have an open mind, you can learn to *create* serendipitous opportunities. When you are truly moved by deep inner conviction, you become a leader, one who cares for a greater cause than personal well-being. Then you will find joy first creeping, and then rushing, into your life.

Is This Book Right for You?

Do you sometimes wonder what you would like to do with your life or whether the career path you are charting is the right one for you? Are you troubled by ethical conflicts in the workplace and in your personal life? Do you have the nagging sense that there is a great deal you have to accomplish and that, somehow, you are not living up to even a fraction of your potential? At odd moments, does a train of thought along the lines of "Is this all there is to life?" spring up unbidden in your mind?

Are you somehow, at some level, dissatisfied with the way things are? This does NOT mean that you have not achieved conventional "success." You very well may have, but you know there is more and can't quite put your finger on it. Is this discomfort strong and growing? Do you have a curious mind and enjoy being challenged by radical ideas and have even come up with a few of your own, or would like to? Are you willing to make the effort to "know thyself"?

If the answer to most of these questions is a resounding yes, then it is likely that you will benefit profoundly from this book.

Here is an even better indicator. The rest of this book discusses topics ranging from freedom to leadership to happiness. There are parables and quotes and strictures. Watch your reactions as you read. Do you find yourself nodding your head? Do you go, "Yes! Yes! That's exactly the way it is"? Do you find yourself so drawn to the material that you cannot put the book down?

If the answer to these questions is also yes, then you are assuredly an excellent candidate for a happy, meaningful life.

WHY CHANGE MATTERS

This book will help you create the internal changes that will resonate far beyond your individual pleasure. Indeed, we can never truly live an ideal life unless we recognize that we are inseparable from others. As Chief Seattle of the Suquamish tribe sagely observed in a purported 1855 letter to President Franklin Pierce, "Humankind has not woven the web of life . . . we are but a part of it. Whatever we do to the web we do to ourselves. All things are bound together . . . all things connect. Whatever befalls the earth, befalls also the children of the earth."

There is little question that we are living in a time of acute change. As always, at such cusps of evolution, the world around us seems to have gone crazy. Government has all but collapsed in many parts of the globe, and its institutions are not held in high regard here. There is breakdown of social order, growing inequality of wealth and opportunity, a seemingly permanent and increasingly disliked underclass, and a degradation of standards in fields ranging from education to popular entertainment.

There is anxiety about the future, seeds of generation conflict, widespread environmental despoliation, and growing polarization of society. Technology has, in many instances, accelerated and exacerbated these trends. On the flip side, there is still a thriving global economy, an increased ability to meet the basic needs of most of humanity, a dynamic international business community, and a growing realization that radical surgery needs to be performed on the existing order of things. Shifts of consciousness can occur with startling rapidity in these days of electronic communication.

I take it for granted that you would like to do your bit, and perhaps a little extra, to leave the world a better place than when you entered it. If you do not, this book is emphatically not for you. Change will have to happen at three levels before the "new era," whatever it is, arrives:

1. **Individual attitudinal change.**
   We will have to recognize that we do not function in isolation, that we have an impact on society and are, in turn, impacted by it. Personal aggrandizement at the expense of everyone else is counterproductive. Greed is neither good for you nor good for society.

2. **Organizational structural change.**
   The world has altered greatly in the last few decades, but our institutions—business, government, religious, and societal—have remained antiquated. The old command-and-control hierarchies are totally unsuited to the present era of instant multilevel communication. Employees seek personal growth and autonomy, citizens

want quick responses to major economic and societal upheavals, and individuals want to revel in their respective individualities. Our current structures and practices are grossly inadequate, mere Band-Aids incapable of coping with severed arteries. Many smaller firms and local governments are experimenting with radically different ways of internal organization. Out of the existing chaos, the butterfly will emerge. The form and color are, as yet, unknown.

3. **Societal value change.**

As long as material accumulation remains the index of success, we will have excess. We will have things galore, but happiness will remain a stranger. Consumption will continue as the measure of well-being, and investment bankers will ingeniously devise ever more convoluted instruments, which may or may not help the organizations on which they are foisted but will certainly ensure themselves a very comfortable early retirement. Too many of our athletes, politicians, and business leaders have become poor role models, interested solely in power and wealth, but we as a society have spawned them through our idolatry. Better leaders will emerge only when we change what we honor. When, for example, a teacher who builds a championship chess team from given-up-for-lost ghetto kids is celebrated more than a drug-ingesting pugilist. There are indeed signs that a backlash has begun, but they are inchoate and diffuse.

This book will get you thinking about all three types of change. Individual attitudinal transformation is, to some extent, under your control and will certainly start happening as you move through the chapters and complete the exercises here. When you reach a position of authority, you can experiment with structural change. The experiment is more likely to be beneficial if you start refining your ideas now. If you reach a position of great prominence, and I hope you do, you might well make a contribution to a change in societal values that will also be affected collectively by the actions of all of the persons you influence. Think of it as the spreading ripples from a stone tossed in a pond, with the ripples growing stronger instead of attenuating.

The First Ripple: Individual Change

Consider this vision:

You wake up in the morning suffused with an ineffable feeling of joy, a deep sense of well-being. You go to work, to a job you love so much that you would pay for the privilege of doing it. You labor intently but are so focused that time flies by unnoticed. At the end of the day you are invigorated, brimming with more energy than when you started. You have a penetrating awareness of the course you are charting, a clear knowledge of your place in the scheme of the universe. Your work feeds this, is congruent with it, and brings great contentment and peace.

You face obstacles, big ones and small ones, perhaps more than your fair share of them. You understand very clearly that their purpose is to test your mettle, to bring out the best in you even as the abrasive whetstone serves to finely hone the knife. So you plow on indomitably, sure of what you want to achieve and yet unconcerned about results. At times it seems as if you are riding the crest of a powerful tidal wave, as if the universe itself is helping you, working with you and through you.

Locked doors open mysteriously. Incredibly fortuitous coincidences oc-cur. You accomplish prodigious feats, feats you would never have imag-ined yourself capable of. Yet it would have been perfectly okay if you had not accomplished them. You accept accolades gracefully but are not swayed by them because you march to the beat of your own drummer.

Your personal life is intensely fulfilling. You are active in a variety of civic, charitable, and political causes and successful in all of them. Your spouse is perfectly compatible with you, a true helpmate in every sense of the word. You beget progeny and your offspring bring great satisfaction. You have a sense of trusteeship toward them. You know that they will chart their own paths and that much of these paths will be forever veiled from your eyes. You are the springboard from which they are launched, and you are glad to bend and provide the greatest thrust that you can. And then you watch with a full heart as they wend their own ways.

So it goes on year after year, each day more perfect than the one before. Your gratitude is so intense that at times it is like a physical ache. Your heart bursts as you thank the universe. What have you done to deserve such good fortune? And when the time comes for you to depart, you do so joy-fully and in peace, achieving identification with the Cosmic Principle, that incredible merging that has been called many things by many peoples but is ultimately indescribable, far beyond the feeble capabilities of language.

A life such as described above is your birthright. You have to reach out and claim it. Will you succeed? I do not know. I do know that the first step toward getting there is recognizing that you **want** to get there. All change begins here, and no change is possible until you have the deep desire for it. It is extremely important that you desperately want to live a life as described above. It is equally impor-tant that you not particularly care whether you do or not. If this sounds like a paradox to you, you are absolutely correct. It is. Remember that all paradoxes are resolved as you reach higher levels of understanding, even the ultimate paradox of all—that which we call life.

Think of that desperate seeker who wanted enlightenment from the Master only to be told that working twice as hard would mean the process of change would take twice as long. That parable contains the secret of personal mastery. You should be steadfast in your pursuit of that goal, but not fixated on it or consumed by it. Your ideal life does not yet exist. You will have to construct it in bits and pieces—somewhat like a jigsaw puzzle.

The Second Ripple: Organizational Change

Contacts are important. Every upwardly mobile professional knows this. How we network with and relate to others in the organizations that surround us determines much of our lives. Politicians know it better than anyone else. Experienced stockbrokers get signing bonuses because they can bring a book of business. Lawyers and lobbyists get hired because of the thickness of their Rolodexes. There are books, courses, and seminars on how to network better. But there is a vast difference between a "networking" contact and a true contact. When we recognize that difference and act accordingly, organizational transformation can begin.

I have always had a problem with the notion that you should cultivate a person based on his—or her—position and the help that you might potentially receive sometime in the future. Apart from the ethical and personal honesty issues involved, consider the enormous amount of time expended in the pursuit of such contacts—the after-hours socializing; the parties and formal affairs; the joining of business, civic, and community organizations to meet the "right" people; and so on.

Suppose it were possible to set up a system whereby you did not have to build a network. Anytime you needed help, a person would appear who had precisely the knowledge and/or resources you required. You can learn to function in this way. There are many prerequisites, the most important being a change in your intentions. Instead of relating to others solely with the purpose of fulfilling a personal agenda, it becomes critical that whatever you are trying to accomplish bring material and spiritual good to a larger community.

Another condition for a change and transformation is that you learn how to let go. You have to relinquish the ego-driven need to be in control, the feeling—in reality, always false—that you are the orchestrator of events. When you have the right mixture of passion for what you want to accomplish, and detachment and acceptance of whatever actually happens, you will be amazed by how locked doors mysteriously swing open. You will find a rescuing army showing up every time you are beleaguered.

> As you proceed, golden opportunities will be strewn across your path, and the power and judgment to properly utilize them will spring up within you. Genial friends will come unbidden to you; sympathetic souls will be drawn to you as the needle is to the magnet; and books and all outward aids that you require will come to you unsought.
>
> —James Allen

In this book you will learn new ways of connecting with people—ways that are powerful and in harmony with your values. Quite a few people have been blown away by the simplicity of the method and the ease with which they have been able to forge strong connections with those to whom they reached out. Some have been well-known figures who are normally unreachable. It may take you a while to tweak this method until it starts working for you, but you will find each exercise eminently useful.

Ultimately, this book will profoundly connect you to others. It is designed to spawn a community. A community dedicated to personal growth and to supporting all those who have started on this quest that is both arduous and exhilarating. Figure out some way to identify and plug into this community and draw strength from it.

The Third Ripple: Societal Change

Leadership is the new fad in our global economy. Innumerable "experts" pontificate on the character of leaders and how to become one. Best sellers identify corporate titans as champions worthy of emulation and reveal their secret—until now—techniques. Military figures, from Attila the Hun through Napoleon to Colin Powell, are being scrutinized for the same reason. It is a burgeoning cottage industry that is rapidly outgrowing its cottage.

The reality is that we have very few leaders in any of our major institutions. We don't have them in education, or government, or business, or unions, or not-for-profits. We have a large number of people in positions of hierarchical authority. They wield great financial and social power, often unwisely. They can certainly impact your life for good or ill. But they are not leaders. They care not if you achieve your potential, and you matter little to them except as a means of helping them achieve their objectives. They have neither overarching visions nor the intuitive knowledge of how this translates into the next step nor the manifest life force that wins dedicated converts to their vision. What they do have is a small coterie of followers who have hitched their stars to them in a calculated bet that this is a route to personal advancement. As John Heider, best-selling author of *The Tao of Leadership*, said:

> True self-interest teaches selflessness. Heaven and earth endure because they are not simply selfish but exist on behalf of all creation. The wise leader, knowing this, keeps egocentricity in check and by doing so becomes even more effective. Enlightened leadership is service, not selfishness. The leader grows more and lasts longer by placing the well-being of all above the well-being of self alone. The paradox is that by being selfless, the leader enhances self.

There are many reasons for this unsatisfactory state of affairs. Our competitive system rewards naked aggression. Our consumption-oriented society equates success with the accumulation of material wealth. Our fragmented worldview perceives leadership as something that can be learned, as a technique that can be deployed.

Leadership is a state of being, not a skill. This is why great leaders have come in all stripes. Their styles have been autocratic and democratic, gentle and brusque, unhurried or frenetically active. Studying these styles will profit you nothing. What will help you is reflection on their deeper qualities. If this reflection produces changes in what you are, then you may be able to use some of their methods with success. Heider has observed that:

> The wise leader's ability does not rest on techniques or gimmicks or set exercises. The method of awareness-of-process applies to all people and all situations. The leader's personal state of consciousness creates a climate

of openness. Center and ground give the leader stability,
flexibility and endurance. Because the leader sees clearly,
the leader can shed light on others.

I have little sympathy for managers who lament that it is impossible to "motivate" workers and who primarily tinker with
various forms of incentives and punishments. Such "motivation"
is okay—maybe—if we are talking about animals in a behavioral-
psychology laboratory. It is demeaning when applied to human
beings. If you become a manager, your function is to figure out
what is demotivating your employees and how to get rid of it.
This is not semantic hairsplitting. It is a completely different
philosophical approach and it has some pretty startling implications.

If you are a parent, a spouse, a friend, a person interested in
social change because you cannot accept the mess our society
is in, then you are—ipso facto—a leader. The exercises in this
book will help you become an authentic leader, not an insipid
imitator.

> There is a soul to an army as well as the individual
> man, and no general can accomplish the full work of his
> army unless he commands the soul of his men, as well as
> their bodies and legs.
>
> —William Tecumseh Sherman

This is equally true of any other organization, including families. The way you command the soul of people is by working on
yourself. By "being" a beacon.

OBSTACLES ON THE PATH TO THE IDEAL LIFE

"IT'S GOOD FOR BUSINESS"

My desk is piled high with books that tout various types of good behavior. Treat the customer right so he/she will keep coming back. Look after your employees so they will treat the customer right and keep him/her coming back. Behave with integrity because—surprise, surprise!—if you do so, your stock price will surely go up.

Every single one of these tomes finds it necessary to justify the behavior by pointing out that if you do this, the company will benefit in terms of revenues, profits, share appreciation, or some similar metric. They make convoluted chains of frequently twisted logic to substantiate their claims and give examples that are far from convincing. But they labor on nevertheless, and the authors are held up as apostles of new and responsible thinking.

What a sorry pass we have come to when simple decent behavior has to be "justified" in terms of some other benefit. What happens if behaving without integrity can get you growth and unparalleled profit? This is frequently the case in many countries with weak legal structures. Do you then jettison integrity?

In my view, you treat the customer right because that is how you like to be treated. You treat your employees well because that is the proper thing to do. You behave with integrity because that is an expression of who and what you are. These are the givens. You DO NOT have to justify or explain or rationalize any of it.

In fact, if you attempt to link your values with external measures like profit, you cheapen them and you discredit your actions.

> We are not here merely to earn a living and to create
> value for our shareholders. We are here to enrich the

world and make it a finer place to live. We will impoverish ourselves if we fail to do so.

—Woodrow Wilson

We have systematically turned over our commercial enterprises to people of overweening greed who use untested economic and behavioral models to justify actions that would otherwise be considered rapacious. It is high time we called a halt to this.

The good news is that there are dozens and dozens of enterprises started by individuals who are profoundly dissatisfied with ruthlessly exploitative business tactics. They are linking up with each other and with social entrepreneurs to create new, more humane business paradigms. It remains to be seen which one will emerge as a new consensus. You are encouraged to join the revolt.

Start such a venture or join one that has already been started. Seed change in the company with which you are already associated. You will enjoy your work more when you are in harmony with the values of the organization you have joined.

THE QUEST FOR "MORE"

One of the most pervasive myths of our society is that "more" will make us "happier." Too few even recognize that this is a myth. Powerful institutions, such as the advertising industry, parade it as fact. Our entire economy is geared to fostering consumption, and the more, the better. Our measures of societal well-being—such as per capita consumption—enshrine this notion. In fact, for most of us, our entire lives are a treadmill of effort to acquire "more"— more money, a bigger house, a more attractive spouse, more power, more fame, more control, more cars and more luxurious cars, more vacation homes, more exclusive and more expensive trinkets. More of anything and everything.

Sometimes the "more" is subtle. More refined and aesthetic pleasures to titillate us. More indulging of ego-driven philanthropic urges. More of the "finer things of life" like friendship, love, freedom, and leisure. More, more, always more. So intricately complex is our ability to play this game that some of us even want "more" simplicity, "more" renunciation. A few of us go to the hilarious end and want "more" asceticism. It is this quest for more that drives us into all of the unfortunate predicaments in which we find ourselves.

> *Where seekest thou? That freedom, friends, this*
> *world*
> *Nor that can give. In books and temples vain*
> *Thy search. Thine only is the hand that holds*
> *The rope that drags thee on. Then cease lament,*
> *Let go thy hold, Sannyasin bold!*
> *Say, Om tat sat, Om!*
>
> —SWAMI VIVEKANANDA

Recognize that there is no problem in seeking more or wanting more or enjoying more. The problem lies in believing that any of this will bring us "more" happiness. The causative link is spurious but, oh, how firmly we believe in it!

This is an important topic and an undercurrent of the entire book. As you do the exercises, you will find that you do not have to struggle to find happiness. It will well up from inside you, unbidden but welcome.

CHAPTER TWO

IT AIN'T REAL!

———— ➤●◄ ————

The first block to personal mastery—and one of the biggest—
is our unquestioned mental models. These are our fixed ideas
of how the world works and how things should or shouldn't
be done. We accept these models so completely that we live our lives
according to them. Everyone has mental models, but we call them
by other names, like "the truth" or "reality" or "the facts." We believe
them absolutely. We have different models for different situations—
for work, for love, for our families. We have dozens of them that we
use, and some of them may actually be in direct conflict with others
and we may not even know it. In fact, much of the stress in our lives
arises from this lack of awareness. But that doesn't stop us from believing that everything our mental models tell us is true.

Here is an example of a mental model about workplace interactions. See if it sounds familiar.

1. My company is very competitive. Everyone
wants to get ahead and will do anything to

do so. The others want me to fail, but they conceal it.

2. My coworkers try to undermine me by being sarcastic, ignoring me, pretending not to hear me, looking through me, boasting about their achievements while underplaying mine, and similar other ways. They are always trying to "use" me.

3. There is a "fast-track" crowd. Persons in this group get more attention from the boss, their expenses are never questioned, they get plum assignments, and their suggestions are always entertained.

4. I would like to be part of this crowd, but I did not go to the right schools and have an accent. I also am too proud to be subservient. I just can't bring myself to laugh at my boss's poor jokes.

5. My coworkers laugh at me and ignore me even though I am better than them in every way.

6. I guess this means that there is no future for me at this company.

7. If that's the case, then I will do the minimum amount of work possible and go

out of my way to bring down the nasty
people. They don't care about me. Why
should I care about them? Perhaps I should
polish up my resumé as well.

Notice how the various parts of this mental model build upon
each other in a downward spiral.

Mental models permeate all our relationships. Here is another example, this time about what a woman feels men find attractive:

1. Men look only for women who are
   physically attractive.

2. Men also like women who are meek and
   submissive.

3. Small is good. Small and curvy is excellent.
   Small, curvy, and not very bright is the best.

4. I am big and intelligent and make my views
   known, so men feel intimidated.

5. I am also not "good looking" in the vacuous
   way men like.

6. When I speak up, they think I am
   "opinionated."

7. I guess men will never be attracted to me. I
   don't fit the "type."

Do you find this funny? Don't laugh! Later, you, too, will articulate the mental models that you use to live your life. Done honestly, your own models will provoke far more mirth than the samples above. Trust me on this.

Here, then, is the first important idea in your transformation: *Your life is a jumble of "mental models." You use them for EVERYTHING.*

You have one model that tells you who to fall in love with, another that evaluates how you are doing in your job, a third that lets you know if your child is growing well, a fourth that spurs you into getting a divorce, a fifth that picks your friends, and so on. You have constructed dozens of these structures over the years and, collectively, they rule your life.

I now further suggest that many of your old mental models do not serve you well. They, and especially the ones that are at odds with each other, are the cause of the angst in your life. But not all mental models are unhelpful. Indeed, I am going to present you with some new ones now that are radically different from anything you have encountered before.

Do not pause and look too critically at the mental models that will be presented to you. Your natural tendency when you come across something that contradicts what you know to be "reality" is to back off and ask, "Is this true?" When you do that, it will not take long for you to come up with hypothetical situations where the model cannot apply and, rather than risk change, you will feel more comfortable rejecting it, heaving a sigh of relief, and reverting to your tried-and-true old models—even though they are the source of your misery.

Don't do this! Let me make it easier for you by admitting right now that the new models I present to you are not "true" either. If you push hard enough, if you penetrate deeply enough, all these models will crumple. But then, so will the ones you are currently using. The ones that you have not subjected to the same scrutiny.

When confronted with a new model, a better question to ask yourself is "Does this new model work better for me than the one I am now using?" If the answer to this is yes, or even maybe, then try it on for size. You can tailor it and tweak it and modify it and make it your own. If, after trying a new mental model for a while, you decide it isn't working well for you, then drop it. Find another. You use *only* what works for *you* in *your* life.

Exercise: My Mental Models

Before you do this first exercise, I urge you to think of yourself as a scientist. The laboratory and the object of study are both yourself. Do this practice as objectively as you can. If you really apply yourself, here is what will happen. Some of the ideas that come out of the exercise will create a rush in your mind. You will feel thrilled as you recognize that you have come face-to-face with something really new. You might start wondering, however, if it can possibly be true. This is the time to STOP READING. At least for a while. Instead, immerse yourself in your excitement, and savor it. Let it grab hold of your imagination. Surrender to it. Bring it up deliberately at stray moments during the day—during your morning ablutions, while waiting for a train or for the traffic lights to change. Remember it while exercising. Let these new ideas become your mental screen saver, popping up after thirty seconds, not every five minutes! Entertain these new ideas until you feel comfortable with them. Then, proceed further.

Now, it's time to start. Take out your journal. On the top of the page write four headings for columns: family, work, love, and self. For the next ten minutes, your pen is not to leave the page, you are not to cross anything out or rewrite or pretty anything up. Just start at the first column and write down the first thing about your family you can think of—something like "My father always criticizes my accomplishments." See where it takes you.

When ten minutes are up, put the journal away. You will use it later. But for now, give yourself credit for having identified some of the more important mental models in your life. You will discover which ones are not working, which are causing you endless grief. You will discard many and modify some. You will adopt new mental models after you have tried them out and are convinced they are right for you.

Through exercises like this one, YOU will create the change in YOUR life. Not me. Not the accounts of others who have done it. All of the latter may help, but only if you accept it. So when you are tempted to not do an exercise—resist the urge! You only get out what you put in!

IT'S NOT REAL!

This is where we start doing some heavy lifting. For some of you, the concept I'm about to introduce will feel like a bomb that blasts the foundations of your life.

You may feel very uncomfortable. You might scoff, dismiss, and deny. Some of you may want to try to claw yourselves back to the old realities where you knew the ground to be firm and unyielding. This may bring some temporary solace, but it will be short-lived. Because when you change your mental models, your world WILL have changed. You CANNOT unlearn an idea that has taken root in your mind.

The idea that can cause all this turmoil is the seemingly innocuous one **that all persons perceive the world differently.**

"Big deal," you think. "Tell me something I don't know." You already accept that different worldviews give life variety; they give us a choice of experiences and enrich us in so many ways. An operatic performance of *Madame Butterfly* can be excruciating torture for one and the height of artistic achievement for another. It is part of our cultural wisdom. As the saying goes, "Do not judge a man till you have walked a month in his moccasins."

This theme appears in countless self-help books and management seminars. It is the bedrock of most workshops on effective negotiation. It is universally recognized as a skill that can be developed, one essential for the success of managers and entrepreneurs.

No one argues against it. It is self-evident. A universal truth.

Like plastique explosive, it can be innocuous. You can hammer plastique, drop it, knead it, shape it, burn it, and maltreat it in ingenious ways and it will remain harmless.

But stick a detonator into it and set it off and KA-BOOM!

This explosion of understanding begins when we turn this familiar concept inside out. In the overwhelming majority of cases where we actively use the idea that persons have different perceptions, we are looking outward. We are examining somebody else.

We seek to understand why a negotiating counterparty can hold such outlandish views and if there is some ground for a mutually beneficial agreement. We "give in" when our significant other wants to see a movie that we have no interest in; we try nevertheless to have a good time, and may even succeed. The refined among us try to sample food and entertainment from different cultures and even develop a taste for them. Travel is a popular way to discover different horizons. We believe that travel is "broadening."

Outside, outside, all outside. We are all looking outside all the time.

It is when we look *inside* that we place the detonator in the plastique. We start to see that if others can have different world-views, then we, ourselves, can change ours. And if we can change our perceptions, then what does that say about what we have always thought of as our true reality? Thus we come to the truly earth-shaking revelation: The world we live in, the one in which we experience such love, angst, and sorrow, IS NOT REAL!!!!!

We invented it. We constructed it out of bits and pieces. We made it out of our mental models and then lived by their dictates. And having done all this, we proceeded to carry on with our lives without ever realizing that our mental models were made up merely of perceptions, not facts. Thus, our lives are not real.

These are deep waters. Some elaboration is in order.

IT'S MERELY A CONSTRUCT

Go back to your journal and read the mental models you wrote down earlier. You may have described your life in bits and pieces such as:

"My boss is a real jerk. No matter how hard I work she unerringly homes in on the one minor item I missed and gives me a lecture on how important it is to make sure I get the details right. When I come up with brilliant ideas, she never acknowledges them. Indeed, she pans them and then tells her boss that she came up with them. That's as good as theft. In fact, it is theft. Unfortunately, the 'higher-ups' really like her because she is personable and very good at flattery.

"I can do her job far better, but the reality is that I will never get a break because she has bad-mouthed me so successfully that everyone thinks I am an incompetent sulk. Life is so unfair!"

"My son got an F in math. Again. And he was out till midnight. Again. He just doesn't seem to be interested in anything anymore. All he does is play those damn shoot-'em-up video games.

The cops called last night because they picked him up drinking beer on the street. A 'warning,' they called it. Why don't they leave him alone and go after the oafs who sell beer to minors?

"The reality is that he is a good kid who's simply too bright for school. He's gotten into some bad company. His friends are into hard drugs, but all he does is have a little beer now and then. That proves he is a good kid. I've just got to support him, be there for him. He'll outgrow those creeps and then there will be no holding him back."

You have dozens, perhaps hundreds, of such "realities." Somehow you have stitched them together into a crazy quilt and together they constitute THE REALITY of your life. Some of the pieces clash with each other, but you put them in anyway and hold them together by force in an uneasy hodgepodge.

Picture your life as a geodesic dome. It has hundreds of polygonal facets, and each one of these is one of the realities you have defined. Together they form an edifice, THE REALITY of your life.

Part of you is dimly aware of this. From time to time, this awareness rises to the surface. You accept that people are different and that they may have perceptions unlike yours that are equally valid. Occasionally, you discard one of your views, thus changing one particular facet. You move from detesting opera to becoming an opera buff. From being Joe Six-pack to an oenophile. From passionately disliking your spouse's relatives to grudging acceptance.

Each of these changes provides evidence to you of your open-mindedness, of your willingness to change. Quite possibly you pat yourself on the back and even look down on friends of yours who are comparatively more rigid. "Relax! Let go!" you hear yourself say. "They also have a valid point of view. Learn to appreciate it."

It never occurs to you that if any one of the facets of your geodesic dome is not true, then maybe NONE of them are.

That, in fact, YOUR LIFE IS NOT REAL, and never has been.

It is a construct. Nothing more. Nothing less. You made it. You live in it. Some parts are good. Many are not. Your life, as you live it and think of it, is simply one of many different possibilities, each of which is equally "real" or equally "unreal."

In the programs I conduct, at around this point utter chaos erupts, swiftly followed by fierce resistance. Quite a few participants feel personally attacked and react strongly. They list their many misfortunes and demand, "How can you say this is not real?" There is strong stuff here. Serious illness and death. Major career reverses. Messy divorces and child-custody battles. Relationship problems with siblings, parents, and others.

You have such issues in your life right now. How dare I say that they are not real?

This is where I become more precise. The hurt you feel—are feeling—IS very real. The life you are living is real.

What you don't realize is that the life you are living is **A** reality. The mistake you are making is that you think it is **THE** reality.

Ponder this for a moment. For several moments. For a day or a week or more. It is not a trivial distinction. It is vitally important. You are a spelunker trapped underground and this is the crevice beckoning you to freedom.

ESCAPE IS POSSIBLE!

Think about it. If your present life is **A** reality, then you can do something about it. You can explore alternates. You can steer in a different direction. You can create a different reality.

If your present life is **THE** reality, you are stuck. Grin and bear it. End of story.

In many cases the distinction is still not clear. You may have far too much invested in your present worldview to give it up so easily. A story will bring it home to you more sharply.

Joey was an immigrant, an ethnic minority, with a thick accent and halting English.

He worked in the maintenance division of a phone company and was very grateful to have a steady income and money he could send home to support his relatives. He worked hard and diligently and soaked up all the knowledge and know-how that he could. But he was acutely aware of his accent and verbal deficiencies.

Joey's foreman, Bill, was white, a tough guy fond of telling off-color jokes. He had a beer belly and a brusque manner. Joey suspected that he was a racist but couldn't prove it.

Joey knew that Bill disliked him. Whenever a really tough job came in, one that involved late-night work in a distant location, Bill would pick Joey. If the work involved complicated splicing, he was certain to ask Joey to head out and stay till it was complete. Not only that, but when other employees were working on jobs like this, Bill would always drop by, check out what they were doing, and crack jokes. He never bothered to look up Joey when he was on a job.

A deep resentment began building up in Joey. It became a knot in his stomach that would not go away. He started sleeping badly and was diagnosed with an ulcer. He would have happily quit, but there weren't too many good alternatives for a person of his age and lack of education. So he simmered, and a permanent frown began to crease his face.

It was against union rules for the foreman to be sending Joey to all of the late jobs. One day, when a particularly messy job came in close to quitting time, Joey tried to protest. "I out last night and two nights before that," he cried. "Bob no go on late call for whole year. Why you no send him?"

"I chose you, buddy, not Bob," said Bill rudely. "Move your ass and get over there as soon as you can. This is a pipe break, so it will probably take all night. Stick with it till it's checked out."

It was the final straw. Joey did the job and then went to file a griev-ance. He was fearful and didn't quite understand the procedure. He was afraid of losing his job because he would be considered uppity, but he could not stand it anymore.

When his motion came before an arbitrator and he was asked to state his case, the floodgates opened. All of his rage, his humiliation, his sense of being picked on unfairly, came pouring out. He spoke emotion-ally and at length.

When he was done, he gazed fiercely at Bill, glad to have gotten it off his chest. He was puzzled to see that Bill did not appear angry. In fact, he looked surprised and contrite.

"Gee, Joey," said Bill, "I had no idea that you felt that way. It must have been real tough for you. Why didn't you tell me before? I send you on all of those tough, messy jobs because you are far and away the best worker I have. When I send you out, I know that it will get done, and done right the first time. I can forget about it.

"When others tackle demanding tasks, I have to drop by and supervise. I never did it with you because you are as good as I am, maybe better. You improve your English and I'll recommend you for a supervisory position."

Joey sat, stunned. Dimly he heard the arbitrator asking him what remedy he would like to ask for and he waved him away. He withdrew the grievance.

Joey decided that he did not want a supervisory role and would take language lessons at his own pace. He liked his job and he liked working with his hands.

Nothing much changed. Joey was still assigned most of the late jobs and virtually all of the really complicated breaks. He was out many nights—more so than all of his coworkers combined. Bill never dropped by to see how he was doing.

But Joey's ulcer disappeared and his eyes started twinkling again and the frown vanished. Bill received complaints about a new workplace hazard—a loud, unmusical noise.

It was Joey singing.

An Alternate Reality

Here is a question for you to ponder: Did Joey really need the arbitration for an "alternate reality" to surface?

Some students in my classes respond with an emphatic yes. Their argument is simple and forceful. If Joey had arbitrarily decided to "live" in the alternate reality, he could have been at risk. What if he had trusted Bill unquestioningly and revealed information to him that Bill then used against him? What if these revelations got him fired? Lambs, even innocent lambs, do get slaughtered.

At this point, participants in my programs are less sure of their ground. Quite a few have thoughtful expressions. They can readily appreciate that Joey is much better off living in a world where Bill has explicit confidence in him, but they are still hung up on whether this is "true."

We press on. I ask if any of them have ever had a terrible boss, a real tyrant who could make life miserable for them for days and weeks on end. A forest of hands goes up. Toxic bosses are not an endangered species.

I then ask them what, in their opinion, is their most important asset. I suggest that it is their ability to be happy. To be fulfilled and content and joyous. Heads nod in agreement. Even those who are not sure this is their "most important" asset readily agree that this capacity is very important. Something to be treasured and guarded.

"Then why," I ask them, "do you take this really precious gift that you have and entrust it to a total jerk like your boss?"

There is always stunned silence. They have never had it framed for them in such a way before.

IT'S DUMB TO GIVE AWAY YOUR HAPPINESS

Think about your own life. Do you choose to live in a reality that is negative, like Joey did? Is there a toxic person in your life who inspires this mental model? Can this person unerringly press all your buttons and leave you quivering with indignation and frustration? Does this annoyance poison your attitude for hours or even days?

What you have just done is taken your most valuable possession, your ability to be happy, and given it to someone else. To someone else who may not be well disposed toward you.

Why would you want to do such a daft fool thing? But you do. Everyone does.

In my classes, after a moment of stunned silence, there is usually quite a hubbub as everyone tries to come to grips with this new way of looking at things. No one argues that this is not a dumb thing to do.

Sooner or later someone ventures, "But it can't be helped! That's the way things are!"

It doesn't take long before someone else interjects, "That's because you have constructed a reality where you can't help it! You don't have to give anyone that power."

I retreat to the sidelines and observe. Managers who attend my programs are a very bright bunch, and it does not take long for them to probe the new model from every angle. The concept of NOT giving anyone this power is intuitively very appealing.

Sooner or later a plaintive voice asks, "Dr. Rao, if I were Joey, how would I go about living in the other reality? How could I avoid giving power over my happiness to someone else?"

That's when the breakthrough happens.

That's when it will happen in your life. When you sincerely ask that question and you really, truly, absolutely want to know the answer.

That is when you experience a paradigm shift, when you slip into a parallel universe that has always been available to you but that you never looked for.

Don't take my word for it. You will discover this for yourself when you try the exercise that follows.

Let's get started.

Exercise: The Alternate Reality

Go back to your mental-models exercise. Pick any one situation that is troubling you right now.

You have constructed a "reality" around your situation. Most likely you believe that this is "the" reality. Explore its many dimensions carefully. Come up with an "alternate reality" for your situation. One that you like a whole lot better. It is not a bad idea to come up with half a dozen such alternate realities from which you will eventually select one.

It is important that YOU, personally, be able to accept the alternate reality you devise.

For example, you may live in a reality where your boss is a real son of a b**** who has it in for you and in whom the milk of human kindness has curdled into an acid powerful enough to be classified a weapon of mass destruction.

One reality you come up with is that your boss is really an angel who is carefully, and lovingly, beneath a gruff exterior, trying to toughen you up for future success.

If this alternate reality is too much for you to swallow, *don't even try.* You *cannot* "con" yourself in this exercise.

However, you may be open to an alternate reality in which your boss is still a grouchy sourpuss, but you are fortunate in having such a confrontation early in your career because it will give you invaluable experience in handling difficult people.

Play around with different plausible scenarios.

Then pick one alternate reality that:

1. Is better than the one you are experiencing right now, and

2. Is one that you can plausibly accept.

For the next week, live "as if" the alternate reality you have selected were true. Behave in accordance with it. Jettison your earlier views and adopt this one.

As you live in this alternate reality, immediately acknowledge and dwell upon every scrap of evidence that it is working. Resolutely ignore the mountain of evidence that you are kidding yourself. You may feel as if you are playacting. You are correct. You are! Eventually you will become the role you are trying to play.

It is important that you are very careful in selecting the role you decide to play. These roles will play an important part in reshaping your reality.

HELPFUL HINTS

The odds are pretty good that the first few times you try this exercise, you will have less than stellar success. Stick with it. Here are some pointers:

1. If you are totally unable to live in your alternate reality, it is very likely that you have picked one that you cannot accept on any level. This is a no-no. Remember that you CANNOT fool yourself. You CANNOT play a con game in this exercise.

   Your challenge is to come up with an alternate reality that you CAN plausibly accept.

   Here is another example: Say your reality is that no one seems to like you. No one calls you for parties, seeks out your company, invites you for dinner, or shows any desire to spend time with you in the evenings or on weekends. They hate you.

   You might pick an alternate reality in which you are incredibly sophisticated and refined and therefore intimidate most others, who are unworthy of you anyway, and you really like spending time by yourself and engaging in intellectual pursuits.

   But can you actually accept that you like being alone and have no regrets? Maybe yes, but probably not.

   You may have more luck with an alternate reality in which people are not cold-shouldering you. They are simply too busy with their own lives and it never occurs to them to include you in any part of it. It's okay for you to take the first step and ask other people to hang out with you. Some will and some won't and that's okay.

2. WRITE IT DOWN! Write down every scrap of evidence that your alternate reality is working. Every scrap of evidence that supports it. If your alternate reality is that you are fortunate in having a toxic boss early in your

career because you will quickly gain the experience you need to be successful later, then write down each painful experience and the lesson you learned. Do not complain and moan: Explicitly label each setback as a learning opportunity and list what you could have done to avoid it and what you will do in the future.

Ignore all thoughts that you are in a dead-end job with no prospects for advancement and shackled to Frankenstein on one of his worst days. What you pay attention to, what you focus on, is what shows up in your life in an increasing quantity.

3. Don't immediately pick the most horrendously important thing bothering you right now. This is a little like deciding to take up jogging and entering a marathon the next week. You need training and much building up of stamina before you can realistically complete a marathon.

Alternate realities are the same. You need practice and the confidence that comes with many successes before you can tackle the really big issues in your life. Start with something important to you, but not one of the big boulders in your life.

For example: Do you live in the reality of an uncaring workplace? One where your coworkers are quick to seek your help and counsel when they are in trouble but where you are by yourself when you are in difficulty?

Try living in a reality where others recognize your caring nature and that is why they come to you for help with their problems. A reality where you are strong enough to deal with situations on your own and that this is obvious to everyone.

LABEL these realities. You may want to call the first one "Uncaring World" and the second "World Where I Can Help." Do you want to live in Uncaring World or in World Where I Can Help? You will discover something wonderful. As you live in one of these realities that you select, you will initially feel as though you are playacting. As you persist, that feeling will go away and it will actually BECOME your new reality.

4. Be gentle with yourself. If you are not having much luck, don't beat yourself over the head and make it one more way in which you can define yourself as a failure. Just construct a whole bunch of different realities according to the guidelines given and try another, and another, and another. Eventually you will find one that works. And soon you will be able to make the others work as well.

Be patient!

Begin with a work situation you are confronting. You will find the results appearing quickly, and almost miraculously. Here is an example:

A three-year associate was constantly told by her boss that she "made him mad" because of what she said, or did, or didn't do. She accepted this and drove herself crazy trying to stop "making him mad." When she did this exercise and discussed it with her classmates, she came to a simple realization. She wasn't driving him mad, he was driving himself mad and blaming her. She didn't have to take responsibility for his anger. However, he was her boss, so she couldn't tell him off either.

So she tried humor. The next time he used his stock phrase, she came back with, "You mean to say I really have that much power? I really can make you hot and bothered? That's cool!" And she looked him in the eye and grinned broadly as she said it.

Within a few weeks he stopped.

Your life is hemmed in by the things you know to be true that aren't. It's time to start setting yourself free.

CHAPTER THREE

It's Mental Chatter, and It Is REAL!

Okay, so the world you live in is not "real." Or rather, it is real but only one of many different possible realities. Certainly the pain you experience, the frustration you feel, the loneliness that comes welling up, the stress that assaults you—these emotions are all real. You have the medical bills to prove it!

The truth is that you were intimately involved in bringing this reality about. We *all* construct our own realities. But why, then, would you create one that is so full of things for which you have no particular affection? How did this happen?

The answer is simple. You did it through your mental chatter without even realizing it. You did it unconsciously. You were playing with matches—lighting them and throwing them aside idly. You just never knew there was gasoline around till the flames engulfed you. Unfortunately, ignorance does not keep gas from igniting.

YOUR CONSTANT COMPANION

You have a companion. One that never, ever leaves you. It sticks with you, staying even closer than your shadow, which forsakes you when you walk indoors and leave the sun. This companion comes right along with you. You cannot shake it loose.

This constant companion is your mental chatter.

If you observe your mind, there is always a monologue going on. It begins the moment you open your eyes in the morning and carries on every single second till you close your eyes at night. More often than you'd like, this chatter prevents you from drifting off to sleep. And when you do finally doze off, it may well make that rest fitful.

Some companion!

Think about what happens to you when you get up. Are you like Cynthia, whose mental chatter goes like this? "Drat! There's that alarm again. I don't want to get up. Do I have to get up? I think I can sleep another ten minutes. I'm going to hit the snooze button. It's cold. Wish I could sleep forever. . . .

"No toothpaste. I told him to get a new tube before he used up the old one, but he forgot again. How inconsiderate. I don't think he loves me anymore. If he did, he wouldn't deliberately aggravate me the way he does. Why does he do it? He didn't use to be like this. At one time he was actually charming. He would hold doors open for me and get me roses and come home early for dinner and pour wine.

"Dinner! That reminds me. He invited his parents for dinner on Saturday and didn't even consult me. How could he? He knows his mother drives me up the wall. I bet she'll go all around the house checking for dust. It'll really make her day if she spots a cobweb. How could anyone possibly be so shallow? I used to wonder how a flibbertigibbet like her could have such a nice son, but I was mistaken. There is a lot of her in him. Why couldn't I see it before? Blast him! He can cook on Saturday. I'm busy. I'll make sure I have to go to work to finish the Hewlett report. That'll show him.

"Look at that blond bimbo crossing the street. Looks just like Gwyneth Paltrow. Why can't I look like Gwyneth Paltrow? Slim and leggy. Every tiny bit of chocolate I eat goes directly to my hips and sticks there. What a hussy. Does she have to show so much leg? I bet her sex life is better than mine. Give it another five years and she'll have a double chin, too. That'll teach her.

"Bet all the guys are nice to her and fall over themselves to do things for her. Why is life so cosmically unfair? There's one just like her in my office. My boss is always reaching for her. What a creep! He has two legs and eight hands. He'd never try that with me. He knows better than that. I'm not that kind of girl.

"Darn, I'm late again. Why won't the darn subway come? I bet the token clerk saw I was in a rush and phoned the motorman to hold up the train. They do that all the time. Why do they always pick on me? Why don't they pick on Ms. Paltrow over there? Oh no, they wouldn't. They'd hurry up the train for her. Why do they always do this when I'm running late?

"I wish she wouldn't lean over me like that. She really should use deodorant. She wouldn't need to if she weren't so overweight. Probably eats fast food every day and lets her kids do the same and they are all obese and sick most of the time and see too many doctors and that's what makes health care so expensive and that's why my premiums keep going up. It's all her fault! She's actually smiling at me. Seems friendly, too. Maybe she's really quite nice, but she is unhealthy and she IS driving my premiums up.

"I can't believe how long it took to get to the office. Got to slow down. Walk in dignified. Would never do to rush in like a schoolgirl. I'll tell J.T. that I had to get the Sandman file from accounting and that's what made me late. Hope he won't ask me for it immediately. It's in my filing cabinet and that would give the game away. Why do I have to make up stories? I wouldn't have to if I looked like Jennifer—all blond and leggy. And look at those skirts. What a tramp. He never challenges her when she walks in half an hour late.

"Have to go to the candidate meeting. Whoever thought that one up? Certified cretin! Said if all of us met the candidate at the same time in a conference room it would save time. Baloney! All of them ask questions to show how smart they are. No one pays attention to the candidate's answers. We never get to know anything about any of the candidates. Not that it matters a bit. He'll just hire whoever he wants. The guys don't have a chance, but they don't know that. He'll give the job to the one with the biggest boobs.

"Lunchtime! Let's get the hell out of here. Lorna stood me up again. Why do I ever bother with her? She says I'm her best friend and never even gives me notice when she can't make it. I wanted to tell her about my mother-in-law coming for dinner. Now I'll have to stew in silence. Maybe Gretchen is free. Let's try her. She told me I should keep Lorna further away. Where's my cell phone? I left it at home. Just the kind of thing that always happens to me. Now . . ."

Does Cynthia's chatter sound familiar? How exhausting! You have your own version of her inner monologue. The wonder is not that you feel stressed and overwhelmed. The wonder is that you are functional at all!

SUE YOUR SURGEON!

Let's suppose that there is a marvelous new gizmo that has just come on the market and you want to be one of the very first to get it. It's a computer chip that will provide you with the very finest in audio and video entertainment and it has to be surgically implanted in your skull. You look forward eagerly to a lifetime of enriching entertainment.

The surgeon screws up. The remote control is tongue operated and it does not work. You cannot change channels. The volume control is busted. It is unpredictable. At times the audio is deafening, so loud it feels as if the entire orchestra has abandoned musical instruments for jackhammers. At others there is barely a whisper.

Sometimes the images and music are vivid and pleasing. At others they are equally sharp but ghastly and frightening. But all too often you experience dull, grainy darkness. A depiction of the rain pouring and pouring and pouring.

You can't turn it off. It explodes into activity when you are trying to sleep and robs you of rest when you need it most. It freely and constantly prevents you from doing what you want. It beguiles you into actions that you almost instantly regret. It gets you into endless trouble.

How long would you put up with this? How long would it take before you were laying out your case to the best malpractice lawyer in town? And how easy would it be to collect and how many zeroes would your award have?

This may seem like a ludicrous example, but you have such a chip embedded in your cranium right now. You accept it because you don't think of it as a chip—you know it as your mind even though it behaves exactly as described above. You think it is "normal."

But now that you know you can change your reality, what do you propose to do about it?

LITTLE DROPPINGS MAKE A MOUNTAIN
OF DUNG: YOUR VOJ AT WORK

When you examine your mental chatter, you will find it is an un-ending stream of noise, but you will also quickly discern that this noise has patterns. One of the most powerful and prevalent is your Voice of Judgment (dubbed VOJ by Michael Ray, emeritus profes-sor of creativity at Stanford Business School). This voice works like a hammer. Sometimes it is a twenty-pound sledgehammer and sometimes it is a jeweler's mallet. Sometimes it pounds you on an anvil and sometimes it merely gives you a mild headache. But it *al-ways* does a darn good job of flattening you.

Sometimes your VOJ puts you down directly. "You're such a dummy," it says. "However did you get a job? You don't deserve it. You'll find some way to screw up. If a jigsaw puzzle had only nine pieces, you'd still get it wrong."

At other times it puts you down more subtly by comparing you, to your disadvantage, with someone else. "Look at him," the voice purrs. "He's so smooth. Never at a loss for a honeyed word or a gracious compliment. Never tongue-tied in a meeting. That's the kind of person who gets promoted. Not a dumb schmuck like you who messes up reading the writing on a PowerPoint slide."

Your VOJ is equally ready to judge others. All others. "Look at her slouching. She's probably had a couple of drinks already. Her nose is red. That proves it. She HAS been drinking."

Or, it can be gracious—"What a charming couple! They must have a wonderful marriage!" But the odds are that most of its pro-nouncements are decidedly negative. Your VOJ has an unerring ability to insinuate itself into the stream of your mental chatter in insidious and negative ways.

When you wake up in the morning and start thinking of all

that you have to get done, before you have taken a single action, your VOJ reminds you of all your weaknesses and failures. As your to-do list begins growing faster than a popcorn bag in a microwave, your VOJ cuts in, remarking, "You'll never get all that done. You're a dope. Why did you have to watch the late show? You've got no self-control. That's why you'll never go anyplace, never accomplish anything."

Your boss is toxic and you are contemplating letting him know that you will not take it anymore and your VOJ pipes up, "That's dumb. Be grateful you have a job. Lots of others would give their right arms to be where you are. You'll rub him the wrong way and he'll fire you and then where will you be?" Your VOJ keeps you trapped in that unhealthy situation.

Over time, the negative judgments start to accumulate. Eventually they form a huge barrier that is placed squarely in front of you on the path to your ideal life. This obstruction is like a coral reef, a strong structure capable of ripping the bottom off the stoutest oceangoing vessel ever made. Yet a coral polyp is a tiny, really tiny, animal that leaves behind a bony skeleton when it dies. Each individual polyp is insignificant and, when taken alone, is of absolutely no consequence. But tens of thousands of polyps, millions of polyps, die and their skeletons bond into that awesome reef.

Your mental chatter and VOJ work exactly like that. Each judgment, each individual chain of thought, may be evanescent, disappearing like each tiny polyp when it dies. But each leaves behind its mark. You have been entertaining an unending stream of mental chatter for all of your waking moments for decades. That stream leaves behind a lot of faint residue. In fact, the accumulation is no longer faint. It is quite a sturdy edifice. As sturdy as any coral reef.

That reef is your reality. It has imprisoned you. And that is how you built it. You never even realized what you were building as you were constructing it. Even if you were dimly aware at times of your tendency toward negativity, you probably dismissed your thoughts as either unimportant or as well-deserved criticisms. And you were partially correct. Each individual coral polyp is unimportant. Each individual thought is inconsequential. But when taken together, they form a massive, destructive reef—the reality of your life.

IT'S A HIJACKING

Have you ever been to a Web site—in all probability one that you should not have visited!—when your browser froze? And then you were attacked by pop-up ads? You click on the cross at the upper-right-hand corner of the screen and nothing happens. Or the screen vanishes but is instantly replaced by another, and another, and another. It is like flailing at a swarm of insects. Sometimes the only way out is to turn off your computer and reboot it. Remember how it felt? These pop-up ads are another pattern our mental chatter takes.

Have you ever considered that you allow yourself to experience this frustration *all* the time? Only, because you call it "Life," you have learned to live with it.

What are these dangerous pop-ups? They are all the ideas, beliefs, habits, and attitudes that you have collected. They came from your parents, your relatives, your teachers, your friends. They came from society and from the media. You picked them up and absorbed them without examination. And now they have taken over your life, intruding constantly without your permission. They have hijacked you!

Where do these pop-up ads, this never-ending stream of them, come from? And is there any link between them and your VOJ? These distracting images come from both inside your mind and from the world around you. That's why their attacks are so powerful and pernicious. You are assaulted on both sides of your perimeter. You have spent decades accumulating a mammoth database of pop-up images and messages and you carry them around with you all the time. This database activates itself automatically many, many times a day and is amplified by the stream of stimuli that come in from the outside. No wonder you feel beat!

Sound unlikely? Let's look more deeply:

Have you ever felt dissatisfied with your physical appearance? Been conscious of a blemish that seems to expand and blot out the sun? Where did you get the notion that if you don't look like Heidi Klum or Brad Pitt, you are inferior? Do you then start to feel depressed (or at the very least mildly unhappy)? You were not born like this—you picked up this kind of thinking along the way.

Is there a toxic person in your life? Perhaps a boss, maybe a relative, or even a "friend"? Does this person have an uncanny ability to leave you a quivering emotional wreck for hours or days or weeks? Why do you hand over your emotional well-being to this person? If this person has hierarchical authority over you, you may have to comply with behavioral demands, but you never have to give up your equanimity. So where did you learn that you have to get all upset and demoralized?

Have you ever looked at someone and felt a stab of envy? Did you want, desperately desire, what that person has? Or, more accurately, what you *think* that person has? Money, power, fame, prestige, cars, houses, boats, or planes? Do you wish that your spouse was as beautiful as theirs or that your kids were as charming, your friends as enchanting? Do you envy their sense of humor, or intelligence, or empathetic gifts? Have you ever made a purchase not because you really wanted it but because you wanted to make a statement to someone else? Where did this desire, and its attendant disquiet, come from?

Are you beset by fears? Do you obsess about losing your spouse, your children, your friends, or your job? Are you terrified of spiders or snakes or one-eyed albino pirates? Do dark spaces or soaring heights make your palms sweat? Or does the thought of going to parties, giving speeches, making presentations, or speaking up for something you believe in that is unpopular scare you silly? Are you numbed by the specter of being stuck in the same dreary career and never achieving the potential you know you have? I regularly hear about all these and many, many more. But where did you pick this up?

These fears are all a result of your conditioning. You picked up this conditioning when you were young, from your parents and teachers and your role models. You saw them all around you in society and they are still broadcast to you from the media that surrounds you. Marketers call it cultural conditioning—your tendency to consume products and think in ways that conform to the broader society you are a part of.

The problem is that this conditioning not only restricts you, it also prevents you from exploring pathways that could lead you to freedom. That is why you feel boxed in and enervated.

Let's go back to your mental chatter. All of the judgments, the comparisons, the put-downs, come from values and beliefs that you picked up in passing. You may have actively studied a few, but for the most part you never examined or questioned them or their underlying assumptions. You used them to create your mental models, hundreds of them. And then your mental chatter used these models to create the reality that you now live in.

That's how it happened. And that's where you live now—in this "reality" that you created. You have, quite literally, been hijacked.

The good news, the really great news, is that once you become aware of what you have unconsciously let happen to you, you can fix it!

We'll get to the fix shortly, but first you have to find out for yourself just how bad your situation is. Do the exercise below for at least two weeks. Really do it. No playing around and pretending you are doing it.

I guarantee that you will be very surprised. Probably unpleasantly so, but that's okay. You are both the doctor and the patient and you have to know how bad the disease is before you start on the cure.

Exercise: What's My Mental Chatter Like?

This exercise helps you become aware of your mental chatter, of the random thoughts that spring to mind throughout your day. You are going to simply observe this chatter without judging it. Especially become aware of your first thoughts in the morning as they are untainted by external events. Look to see if there are either patterns, repeated single thoughts, or simply random, disjointed thoughts that spring up unbidden, vanishing as swiftly as they arise.

During the day, carry around your journal or a file, or notebook, or a sheet of paper. Categorize the types of mind chatter that assault or beguile. Do this for at least two weeks. Are there wild flights of fancy? Elaborate escapist dreams? If so, try to be specific about exactly what types of accomplishments you fantasize about. Sports? Business? Entertainment? Are others involved? How? Create as many categories as you need to, but you will probably find it unwieldy to deal with more than six to eight.

As you do this, try to become aware of any emotional undertone(s). An emotional undertone is a feeling that persists at a gut level, below your conscious stream of chatter. Common ones are sadness, a sense of being overwhelmed, fear, frustration and dissatisfaction, and so on. Your emotional undertone can also be positive, such as quiet confidence or deep peace. Is there one dominant feeling throughout the day, or are there two or three? Are these undertones equally strong—or weak? Do they change from day to day, or are they reasonably constant? Are they generally negative—anger, self-doubt, anxiety, worry, etc.—or are they generally positive—hopeful, loving, or confident? You can define positive or negative in any way you wish. How do these undertones affect your behavior? Are you a better performer at some task when a particular undertone is in charge? Do you tend to flare up when another one holds sway?

Do these undertones tend to disappear when you start noticing them? What does this tell you? Does the intensity of the emotion decrease simply because you become consciously aware of it?

Be sure to note if you run yourself down, and if you are constantly criticizing yourself. Do you treat yourself this way frequently, or occasionally, or not at all? If you do run yourself down, do you also blame others or feel victimized by external events?

Finally, notice when external stimuli hijack your mental state. Does a news broadcast lead you to consider the state of the world? How do you react? Did you react emotionally, with fear or concern or anger? Did you feel depressed or powerless? Try to note when external events create your emotional state. Notice when distractions push and pull at your well-being. Did an advertisement with glamorous people remind you of a relationship breakup and lead you to despondency? Did a phone call from a friend remind you of a weekend expedition you have planned and uplift you immediately?

This may seem like a simple exercise, but it is not as easy as it first appears. I guarantee you that there will be long stretches where you simply forget to note your mind chatter and just let it carry you away. It will help if you have—or get—one of those digital watches that can be set to beep every hour or half hour. Each time you hear the beep, become aware of your mind chatter. The beep will help you to remind yourself to get back into observation mode. You can also train yourself to use random events—phone calls, e-mail bleeps, greetings from friends, etc.—as prompts to return to your observations. Persist. Practice will make you better.

Do this exercise for two weeks. You may actually want to do it for longer, but two weeks will give you enough knowledge to get started on making changes.

What You Will Get from This Practice

Most people find this exercise extremely revelatory. Even those who have had exposure to the philosophical underpinnings of Yoga or Eastern meditation learn a lot.

People are startled by how active their Voice of Judgment is, how often they put themselves down and are severely critical of others. They're surprised by how many snap judgments they make about trivial things, like, "That ice-cream flavor looks sickly pink"—or more serious matters like, "This is the third time he has stood me up. He doesn't care. I'll break off with him." The VOJ can be anything from 20 percent to 60 percent of your mental chatter, and negative judgments typically outweigh positive ones by anywhere from two to one to ten to one.

Since you build mental models out of your mental chatter, when you become aware of your judgments and emotional distractions, you gain some much needed control over your life. You get to decide for yourself whether you are going to build a reality on the foundation of a negative judgment.

HELPFUL HINTS

1. You may feel that you register only 10 percent of your thoughts. You are wrong. It is unlikely that you are aware of even 0.000001 percent of your thoughts. There are simply too many of them, and they change too rapidly, and you forget that you are supposed to be aware of them most of the time. Throw a stone on a wasps' nest and then try to count the insects as they come swarming out! Recording mental chatter is exactly like that.

   That's the bad news. The good news is that even the most minimal level of awareness creates profound change. If you persist sincerely for a few weeks, you *will* become aware of the amount of self-flagellation you indulge in. You will be shocked by the quantity and variety of the negative voices of judgment you harbor.

2. Do not beat yourself up when you note the negativity of your thinking. Doing so simply creates yet another stream of mental chatter for you to record. Remember that in this exercise, you are simply a recorder. A scribe. Try to note your chatter dispassionately. That's all you do at this stage.

3. Some of your mental chatter may turn out to be with minimal emotional undertones. You may see yourself occupied by something neutral such as making to-do lists, planning your day, or organizing your work. That's fine. Just note it.

4. Especially be aware of your emotional tenor during the day and how these mental states work together with your

mental chatter. You may find that negative judgments tend to produce emotional downs, while thoughts of gratitude produce an elevation of spirits.

Do this exercise for at least two weeks, but don't stop there. Try to get to the point where you constantly become aware of your mental chatter. Every time you are confronted with some life event that generates strong feelings, become conscious of it immediately. The very act of observing it changes your mental chatter. Shoplifting drops dramatically when department stores install surveillance cameras and post signs that they have done so. In the same manner, your mental chatter is less able to take you down destructive paths when you consciously become aware of it.

I invite you to discover this for yourself.

CHAPTER FOUR

YOU CAN'T KILL IT AND IT WON'T SHUT UP! THE WITNESS IS YOUR SALVATION

—⇒•⇐—

Y ou have begun to see how your mental models and chatter have created the "reality" in which you now find yourself. Remember that you absorbed mental models from your parents, teachers, friends, society, the media, and other sources. For the most part, you accepted them unquestioningly. You have examined very few of the assumptions that underpin these models and have tested even fewer. So blissful is your ignorance that you are not even aware that you are using mental models, and are doing so virtually *all* the time.

Your mental chatter picks up these models and applies them to your life. It is very much a two-way street: The models influence your chatter and your chatter modifies your mental models. Together, through constant interaction, they create *the reality* of your life—or, at least, your perception of it.

Your Reality Is Between Your Ears

Alex came to work late that morning and his thoughts were feverish. It was confirmed. The CEO would have to undergo a quadruple bypass. He would retire. Even the CEO did not know this. Alex knew it because he had just spent an hour with the CEO's wife and the lady was implacable in her decision. She intended to have her husband home and free of the tension that had just laid him low for the second time.

Alex was the logical choice for the job. He knew the company cold, was running its largest division, had few overt enemies, and had exceeded his numbers handsomely for the last three years. But age was against him. He was only three years younger than the disabled leader, while Nick was a dozen years younger.

Nick had been his protégé. Alex had picked him from the M.B.A. associates pool and taken him under his wing. He had recognized the younger man's talent and drive and had given him more and more responsibility. He intended to promote Nick to his position when he moved up, as he had done three times before. It had not worked out that way. It turned out that Nick had forged independent links with board members, and he was plucked out from under his care and made head of all manufacturing, reporting directly to the CEO. And now Nick was being considered for the top post. It was a bitter pill, and Alex felt the bile rise up in him.

Amy, his secretary, was in, and she hurriedly finished a conversation as she spotted him. She looked furtive and his antennae went up. "Who was that?" he queried. "It was nothing important," she said, brushing him off. Amy had been with him for a decade, and Alex would have trusted her with his life. She was mad at him right now. She wanted to do an executive M.B.A., but those programs cost upward of $100,000 and she was not eligible. She asked him to use his influence to push it through human resources anyway, but that would have involved cashing in too many chips and he declined. He had already put in the paper-

work to create a special position for her that would have made her eligible for the executive M.B.A., but she did not know this.

Alex picked up a contract, went to the photocopy machine, and surreptitiously yanked the plug. Then he walked over to Amy, told her the machine was not working, and asked her to make him a copy immediately. As she turned the corner, he leaned casually over her desk and hit the memory button on the phone. The last incoming call and the time it came in popped into view. It was Nick! She had been talking with Nick! The maneuvering had begun!

He could not believe that Amy would work against him, so he decided to give her a chance to explain. "I need to talk with Nick about getting the Argentine order out on time," he said as she gave him the contract back with a copy. "Have you spoken with him recently? Do you know where he is?" He noted idly that the copy was neatly stapled. She knew it irritated him to have pages not aligned. That was what he liked about her—the hundreds of small ways in which she made his life easier. "No," she said, and he detected the fluster in her voice. "Do you want me to call his office?"

"Don't bother," he said. "I'll get him at the staff meeting tomorrow."

Her betrayal was a sharp pain in his gut, so sharp he wondered if he was having a heart attack. "How could she do this to me?" Alex fumed silently. "After all that I've done for her." With cold, controlled rage he called human resources and asked that the new position be put on hold. It would take him some time but he intended to see that Amy was fired. For cause and with no compensation. That's what traitors deserved. He remembered ruefully that the Prince had never had friends. Machiavelli sure had it right.

Time to get to work, to reach for the position that was rightfully his. He started calling the directors individually, intending to make them social calls that would nevertheless leave them with the certitude that he *was the right man for the job. The first four he called were all out, and he felt a cold suspicion harden in his stomach.*

When the fifth director Alex called was also out, he tried subterfuge. He knew all the secretaries. He made it a point to know all of them and the names of their spouses and where their kids went to school. It had helped him more than once. "Hi, Emily," he said casually, "I really need to speak with Bob, and the last cell conversation I had with him was terrible. Kept fading in and out. Is there a land line where he is that I can use to get him?" She gave it to him. He did the same with the next two.

He looked up the phone numbers in a reverse directory and the truth hit him like a freight train. They were all at the law firm the company used. There was a board of directors meeting going on and he had not been invited! He had not even been informed! He called Nick's office, in a frenzy, and tried the same ploy.

Nick was there, too! Nick had been invited to the board meeting, and he had not. It could mean only one thing. He had been outmaneuvered up and down the line. The battle was over before it was joined. How could they do this to him? He had toiled so hard for the company. Given it so many evenings and weekends, forsaken so many vacation days. How could Nick face himself in the mirror? Nick knew how much he wanted the job, and now he had thrown him over without a second thought. A white-hot rage consumed him and made him temporarily immobile with pain.

Alex had one final weapon. He had nursed it secretly for years and the time had come to use it. When he recovered, he moved to his computer and started typing an anonymous letter. Nick had lied on his resumé. He had never finished college. There was no doubt about it—he had sent away for the actual transcript and it clearly showed that Nick had not met the requirements.

The background check had not revealed this because Nick had finished his M.B.A. at a top school and the agency had verified only the fi-

nal degree. The deception had occurred earlier. He wondered if the school would withdraw the M.B.A. when it discovered that he had lied on the application. He finished typing and folded the sheet into an envelope, using his handkerchief to avoid getting fingerprints on it. He addressed it in block letters, using a pencil, stamped it, and put it in his pocket. He would mail it in the evening at a mailbox on the other side of town. If Nick was knocked out, there was still hope for him, but the thrill had gone. He, too, intended to retire soon. He did not wish to stay in a place where he was not appreciated, where they were ready to toss him out so cavalierly.

There was a knock on the door. It was Amy bearing a summons from the CEO. He was needed urgently. With a wry grin, he followed her. They wanted him out immediately. He wondered if his office would be sealed once he left the building or if they would do him the courtesy of letting him leave at his leisure. Amy followed him, prattling brightly, and her effervescence, which used to buoy him, grated harshly. He stifled his hate and smiled politely.

They reached the CEO's favorite restaurant and went up the elevator to the private dining room. He composed himself with an effort of will. He would not let them see him break down.

Amy held the door open for him and he strode in. The assembled group burst into a refrain of "Happy Birthday" and then clustered around him, pumping his hand in congratulations. There had been a board meeting and the CEO had resigned. Nick had proposed him for the new CEO and it had been approved unanimously. "I can't tell you how much I look forward to working with you once more," said Nick, and his eyes were moist. "It will be like old times again. Let's get them good." That was their slang for besting competitors. It was their private communication. Nick still remembered!

The CEO came over. He was in a wheelchair and reached up to pat Alex on the shoulder. He was going in for surgery the next day and did not want any uncertainty to disquiet the analysts or the managers of the hedge funds who were stocking up. "Your birthday is next week, but I didn't think you would mind celebrating early with me," he said roguishly as he poked him in the midriff.

Alex's mind was in a whirl as he listened to the outpouring of support. He reached inside his coat and drew out the letter he had typed. With shaking fingers he tore it into small pieces and threw it into the trash bin. "What was that?" Amy asked him curiously. She had arranged for his favorite appetizers, and his entrée was being specially delivered. "Nothing important," he said.

Don't be in a hurry to proclaim that you are different from that executive. Don't be so sure that you are not either being completely fooled or that you are wildly misinterpreting your own situation, as he did. Is it possible, just possible, that the waves of feelings that overcome you might have their roots in some faulty assumptions? It does not matter whether or not you were deliberately deceived or you simply misread your situation. What matters is what reactions these "untruths" produce in you and what actions you take based on them.

Look at your own life and see if you, too, have fallen into this mental trap. Say your boss brushes past you brusquely and you immediately jump to the conclusion that he is angry with you for some reason and thus must be dissatisfied with your work. Or your spouse seems distant and you know for certain that it is because he is having an office romance. Your best friend forgot your birthday and you know it's because she does not like you anymore. Your coworker yawns during your presentation and you realize that he is clearly working behind the scenes, trying to shoot down your project. There is a huddle at the coffee machine that goes silent as you approach and you know that they were making snide comments about you. The list of what we "know" is endless.

The notion that you can manufacture emotions in response to external stimuli and be moved by them is not new to you. You know this happens every time you are touched by a novel like *Love Story* or *The Bridges of Madison County,* or moved by a film like *Casablanca* or *Forrest Gump,* or deliciously scared by movies like *Psycho* or *The Exorcist.*

Yet because you know that the novels are fiction and the movies are fantasies, you go along for the ride, retaining some emotional control. The same principle holds true in life. There, too, you go along for the ride, but this time it is involuntary. Since you see life as "reality," you don't have the same recognition that you are allowing external events to create your emotional condition. Instead, your trust in the make-believe "reality" of your inaccurate interpretation of events causes you to cede control simply because you don't believe you have any.

The executive in the story may have been an extreme case. But all of us are busy doing the same thing—we just don't acknowledge it. We don't even know it.

DOES YOUR REALITY WORK FOR YOU?

Now that you've begun to see how you have constructed your reality and are busy living in it, you can go to the next step and ask yourself if you are satisfied with your construction. Go back to the description of an ideal life in Chapter 1. Is this what you have created? If so, bravo! Drop this book and do something useful. Take a walk. Play tennis. See the sunset.

But the odds are very good that you are not completely satisfied with what you have created. Indeed, the chances are that you are acutely *dissatisfied* with much of what you have brought into being as a result of living in the "reality between your ears."

Try thinking of your negative or false realities as boulders that you carry around with you every day—every minute of every day. Think of how much time you spend overwhelmingly preoccupied with what others think of you, and the ever-so-crafty ways in which you try to influence their opinion of you. Think of your desperate attempts to achieve career success, and the numbing realization that each step up the ladder leads you to a plateau where more is demanded of you and the satisfaction you initially felt swiftly vanishes. Your frantic efforts not only to hold on to what you have but to increase your success often come with the sad realization that you are constantly dropping balls as you try to juggle too many of them.

Most of all, think about the Voice of Judgment that is with you all the time and that you try to drown out with incessant activity. Think about your despair as you realize that there is a song within you that you don't know how to bring out, and time is fleeting by.

As you contemplate all this, can you honestly say that your mental reality works for you? Probably not.

By Golly! I'll Stop That Mental Chatter!

As the truth about mental chatter and the way in which it shapes our world sinks in, rebellion arises. It's often at this point in a class or a seminar that my students will thank me for pointing out the problem. They think they have the solution and sally forth to do battle with their mental chatter and eradicate it.

They are logical people. Since mental chatter has created the problem, they say, the obvious thing to do is to slay it. Kill it. Make it kaput. The same thought may have occurred to you. Go ahead. Try it. Exterminate this insidious and noisy monster. Root it out. Do it now.

I strongly encourage you to attempt quelling your mental chatter. It will not take you too long to discover what others have— that *you cannot!*

The truth is that it is impossible to extinguish your mental chatter. Any attempt to stanch its flow paradoxically energizes it and increases its intensity. Think of a wild horse in a field. Sometimes it is running around and sometimes it is standing quietly. Just try to saddle it and it explodes into violent activity as it rushes to escape. That is exactly the situation you face. You cannot dam a river in flood. You cannot stop your mental chatter.

That's the bad news.

AN INCREDIBLY FERTILE PLOT OF LAND

That's also the good news, because your mental chatter is actually not the enemy even though it may appear so. It has worked against your interests only because you have let it. You have been so unaware of its presence that you have largely ignored it. In doing so, you've given it free rein to merrily create the haphazard structure of your life.

Imagine that you have a fertile plot of land. The topsoil is deep, several feet of it. It is rich in nutrients. There is plenty of sun and lots of water. There are no deadly frosts or searing heat waves. You clear the plot and turn the soil in it because you want a nice vegetable garden.

Something happens and you have to go away for a couple of months. When you come back, you find a profusion of greenery—mostly weeds—in your field. The thicket is so dense that you can't even see the ground anymore. Now imagine what you would find if you had gone away for several *years*. How totally impenetrable the forest would be, how unusable your land.

Your mind is like that fertile plot. It *will* nurture growth. You can't stop it. There is nothing you can do about it. You cannot prevent it. It absolutely *will* produce vegetation.

What you *can* do is influence *what* it brings forth. If you plant vegetables in neat rows, pluck out the weeds as soon as they thrust their heads aboveground, keep out stray animals, and so on, you will find yourself with a profusion of healthy vegetables—probably far more than you can consume yourself. You will enjoy such plentitude that you can freely give them away to friends and neighbors. Your abundance will sustain many.

Your life can be like that plot of land. It all starts with your mind.

You have been AWOL from your fertile acreage for years, probably decades. Why are you surprised that your mind has produced a tightly packed mess of flora? Be grateful that in that mess there are still some useful plants. Express your gratitude for whatever you find that sustains you and then set about straightening out your garden.

AWARENESS: THE ONLY TOOL YOU WILL EVER NEED

How do you prevent weeds from entrenching themselves in your garden? How do you prevent yourself from being swept away by windstorms of despair and gusts of exultation? The method is simple, although you may not find it easy. You use a tool called "awareness," and it is all you will ever need.

When you become conscious of what you are permitting to germinate inside you, something amazing happens. Almost effortlessly, the weeds in your life will wither simply by exposing them to the light of awareness.

Awareness gives you emotional control. Imagine that you are watching the famous shower scene in the movie *Psycho*. The character played by Janet Leigh revels in the hot flow of water. The character played by Anthony Perkins creeps forward with the knife. At that exact instant, however, a voice whispers in your ear, "It's only a stream of pictures projected on a curved white screen at the rate of fifty frames a second."

Bang! The tension dissipates immediately.

It is exactly the same with your mental chatter. The moment you become aware of the onset of the Voice of Judgment, an outward distraction, or any emotional undertone of anger, hate, or fear, your conscious awareness will immediately diminish it. To use this tool effectively, however, you will need a special companion.

THE WITNESS: THE BEST FRIEND YOU WILL EVER HAVE

Remember the exercise where you dispassionately observed your mental chatter and categorized it? The guy who was observing it is the Witness. The Witness is universal. You will probably find it convenient to think of the Witness as the same sex that you are. Cultivate him or her assiduously because you will never have a truer friend or one who will do you more good.

The Witness is a dispassionate observer. He never passes judgment. He never condemns or compliments. He merely observes, and his observations are acute. The Witness knows all and clearly understands the convoluted games you play with yourself. For example, he notes when you are fooling yourself. "He is gorging on pizza again despite having sworn to lose weight," he tells you. "Now he is beating himself up for not having the willpower to stick to his diet. Now he is coming up with the clever rationalization that he had to eat because he was with a client. Now he realizes that he is trying to rationalize and is even angrier. He is mad at himself for not staying away from the pizza and even madder at himself for trying to rationalize it. Now he is resolving never to do it again and he also realizes that he has made this same resolution many times in the past week alone. Now he is sinking into despair because he thinks he is a failure and will never amount to anything if he cannot do a simple thing like lay off the fatty food. Now he is bawling and . . ." And so it goes.

When you cultivate your Witness, a strange thing happens. You feel as if you are living life on two parallel tracks. You are doing things as you normally do, yet you are also watching yourself do the things you normally do. Initially it is an eerie feeling and you may feel quite uncomfortable. If you can hold on to the Witness for a few minutes at a time, you are doing well, very well. Quite often the Witness disappears in seconds. It's natural for our minds to resist exposure to the light.

The advantage of making friends with your Witness is that he shows you with absolute clarity the many ways in which you frustrate yourself and act in self-defeating ways. You have already seen an example of this when you observed your mental chatter. If you have done this exercise sincerely and with care, you will notice that your mental chatter has already changed. It is less destructive than before. It can still drag you off on journeys that you do not want to undertake, but not quite as easily.

Slowly, very slowly, you are beginning to turn your life around. That's what your Witness will do for you and that's why he is your best friend, the friend you ought to nurture and care for more than any other.

THE WITNESS AND YOUR MENTAL MODELS

You pick up your mental models from all around you—from the media, from advertising, from friends and relatives, from observation. All too often you pick up these ideas and images of the way life is supposed to be without even knowing you have done so.

Do you have notions of romance and of two hearts joining together and beating as one and living happily ever after? From where did you get them? You got them from Hollywood—or Bollywood. And you have undoubtedly suffered your share of angst as you tried to make your life conform to these mental models.

You are running yourself ragged and buying ever more stuff because an extraordinarily sophisticated advertising industry is constantly bombarding you with messages stressing that happiness comes from consumption.

You are attracted to a woman and she resists all your advances, so you seek advice from your friend. He suggests bombarding her with gifts—rare orchids, imported chocolates, vintage wines, expensive accessories. You try it and it works. You repeat this with the next woman you want to date. You have just internalized a model of "how to get a date." You have also internalized, without explicitly recognizing it, "what women look for when deciding if they want to go on a date." This is now a part of your world. The question is, do you WANT this to be a part of your world?

Relations with your boss are not the greatest. You talk to a trusted colleague about this and he listens sympathetically. He points out that you are being systematically sidelined and can expect to be fired soon if you don't take action now. He shows you how to form a relationship with higher-level executives and undercut your boss. It works. You get promoted and your boss gets fired. You have now accepted a model of "how to get ahead at work," and simultaneously, without explicitly recognizing it, have also accepted "how the corporate game is played." Once again, the question is, would you like this to be a part of your life?

These mental models are not the source of our problems. But our lack of awareness of them is. When we aren't conscious of their power, we frequently pick up mental models that we do not want, ones that don't reflect our values. Things become further muddled because many of our values are themselves mental models that we picked up unquestioningly. That is how we built our lopsided and crazy world.

This is where the Witness comes to the rescue. The Witness calmly exposes us—and our models—to ourselves. "He is sending her expensive gifts that he cannot afford," he says. "He believes that all women can be enticed this way." Or, "He is undercutting his boss by devious methods. He thinks this is how companies operate."

When bluntly laid out like this, it makes you pause. You think about what you are letting into your mental DNA. Gradually, you get to the point where you can control what you are consciously comfortable with letting into your mind.

And that is how you start straightening out your life.

Exercise: Present Moment Awareness

This exercise will bring your Witness to life. Pick one day and commit to doing *all* your activities deliberately and unhurriedly. Focus intently on whatever you are doing. No multitasking allowed. No talking on your cell phone while you scan the *Wall Street Journal* and check your e-mail. For most of us, life has become one huge, frantic rush. Slow it down. Firmly and deliberately.

If you are working on a project, just do it one step at a time. Concentrate on each stage and be methodical. I did say unhurriedly. I did not say slowly. Be aware when your mental chatter cuts in with distracting thoughts of how much you have to do, the consequences riding on what you are doing, or how the world is going to end if you don't get your work done perfectly and on time.

Try to let go of your mental model of how you should be and the results that should follow from your actions. Let it all go. Each time your mental chatter carries you away, just gently detach yourself and come back to the task at hand. Breathe slowly, deeply, and evenly. Try to get to twelve breaths a minute or slower. Just being aware of your slow breathing will largely stymie your mental chatter.

This is especially important when you are speaking with someone. *Do not* get involved in your mental chatter, with the wonderful reply you are going to make, with the image of yourself you are trying to project, and so on. Focus on the other person and what he/she is saying. Observe the expression on his/her face. *Really* notice the other person. *Really* listen to what he/she is saying. *Remove* yourself from the picture.

Imagine, vividly, that your life is like an hourglass. The sand above represents all the things you have to do, all the things that are pressing on you and clamoring for your attention. No matter how much you shake and agitate the hourglass, only one grain at a time goes through the narrow neck.

That grain is the task at hand. Focus on it.

I did ask you to bring this focus to all of your activities. If you succeed, you will have achieved a level of personal mastery so great that you certainly do not need this book! But I don't expect you to succeed. I do know that if you try to do it as much as you can, you will be astonished by the results. You will get far more done with much less stress. Once you start to sample some of these amazing changes, you will want to do this exercise as often as you possibly can.

Exercise: Eating Mindfully

Here's another exercise to try. It's somewhat easier than the first one because it is anchored to one discrete activity. It is a great companion to—not a substitute for—the previous awareness exercise.

Eating is a sacred act. Pause to think about this. What you ingest—by some miracle that we do not fully fathom—is converted into bone and muscle and sinew. It gives you energy and the life force that enables you to pursue your goals.

For seven consecutive days eat at least one meal in *total silence*. No reading of newspapers or magazines. No television, radio, or stereo to provide background chatter. No friends, colleagues, relatives, or anyone else to shoot the breeze with. Just you and your food.

Pay close attention to the act of eating. Do not wolf down your meal. Chew slowly and thoughtfully. Be aware of each fork—or spoon—that you bring to your mouth. Notice the saliva coming forth to mingle with the food. Feel your teeth cutting and chewing. Recognize the subtle flavors—you will be surprised by how many there are. Bring the same awareness to whatever you drink. You might want to shut your eyes after each mouthful—or sip—as an aid to awareness.

Pay attention to the reactions of your body. Be aware of the pangs of hunger. When do they get sated? Do you continue eating after this point?

If you are married or have a significant other, feel free to involve them in this exercise. You can both do it in companionable silence and compare notes later. It's also okay if you just want to do it by yourself. Recognize that our society does not make it easy to conduct an experiment such as this. There will be eyebrows raised if you try it in public spaces like restaurants or cafeterias. Some of you will be bothered by this, others will not. Pick the times and arrange the circumstances so you are most comfortable.

There is frequently resistance to this exercise for various reasons. It feels "unnatural," "It's the only time I get to spend with my husband and I value our conversation," "I have meetings every day of the week," and so on. Recognize that these are flimsy excuses and try to bore down on where the resistance is coming from. Being with oneself can be frightening; so don't berate yourself if you still find it difficult.

For those of you who have issues with food, this can be a tremendously powerful exercise. If you constantly find yourself breaking your diet, try the following: Count how many times you normally chew your food before you swallow it, and double the number.

Try to chew each mouthful thirty times before sending it down your esophagus. This is tough, really tough. Long before you get there, your food will have dissolved into a liquid. Hold the liquid till you reach thirty and then send it down. You will find that the best way is to keep the food on one side of your mouth and chew it a little at a time until you reach the magic number thirty.

You will also find a dramatic reduction in your food intake if you do this conscientiously. It's a great help for those who want to lose weight!

Note: Increase the number of chews—up to thirty times—*only* if you have issues with food and would like to experiment with this technique/tool. It is *not* required of everyone. What is necessary is that you are mindful during the act of eating.

COMMON REACTIONS AND HELPFUL HINTS FOR THESE TWO AWARENESS EXERCISES

Most of us—indeed, practically all of us—will find it impossible to be mindful all the time. Don't berate yourself if you lose the Witness repeatedly. This is perfectly normal. If you can summon the Witness a couple of dozen times a day when you start, and even if he stays with you for just a few minutes each time, you are doing wonderfully well. You will immediately notice that you are less carried away by your thoughts on journeys you do not wish to undertake.

If the Witness remains with you when you are in the grip of strong emotions, you are doing even better. You will notice that when you are with the Witness, your strong emotions are a lot less tumultuous and much less capable of sweeping you away.

Some people feel an inordinate amount of resistance to the eating-mindfully exercise. It is very deeply rooted and goes beyond the simple reluctance to give up time with friends or a significant other. If you find this is the case with you, just note it. Do use gentle force on yourself to try it, but not more than that. Keep doing it until the resistance goes away. This could take weeks. In rare cases, it could take longer.

Quite a few report that they feel very queasy eating certain foods as they think of the origins of the items they put into their mouths. If this happens to you, change your diet to something that does not produce such a reaction. In any event, fruits and vegetables are good for you!

Commonly, people notice that they become full long before their plate is empty. If you eat slowly and pay attention to your food, your body tells you when it has had enough. In most cases, this is after you have eaten a fraction of what you normally consume. Try taking smaller portions. Sustained weight loss occurs frequently and for many is a delightful byproduct of this exercise.

Trying to be mindful all the time is extremely challenging, and it is common to feel overwhelmed by the sheer magnitude of the undertaking. If you start feeling beleaguered, simplify your practice. Pick a couple of time slots of no more than ten to fifteen minutes' duration and do your practice in this selected way. As you become more comfortable, you can gradually increase the times.

YOUR MIND IS PRECIOUS: PROTECT IT!

As your practice continues, your Witness grows stronger. He or she will become your protector. Imagine that you live in a high-crime area. There is a knock on your door. You engage the security chain and peer out. There are unsavory characters outside. You smell alcohol and marijuana, you see knives and baseball bats.

How fast would you slam the door? How dearly would you guard that entrance?

You need to protect your mind with the same ferocity as you protect your body. You have to be mindful of what you let in. Your Witness will help you observe who crosses your mental threshold. Do you watch titillating "reality" shows and violent crime dramas? What do those programs tell you about "how the world really is"? Is this what you want to believe? What kind of emotional space do they leave you in? Relaxed, at peace, and full of joy and wonder? Or hyped up, strung out, breathing fast, and filled with tension? Is your forehead furrowed or smooth? Are your muscles tight or relaxed? Simply asking yourself such questions on a consistent basis will produce a dramatic change in what you expose yourself to. The Witness will see to that.

The physician who became better known as Swami Sivananda once remarked, "It is better to allow yourself to be cut with a sharp knife than to let a wrong thought in your mind."

The Witness is your guard. The one who alerts you to the attackers who are trying to breach your walls and enter. Pay attention to your Witness. There is no one else looking out for you.

Try to remember that when you are dealing with your mental chatter, force does not work—that it is, in fact, counterproductive. The more you try to eliminate particular trains of thought, the more they will take you away on unwanted journeys. Trying to suppress them energizes them.

But observation accomplishes what force cannot. The Witness is a remarkable pacifier. Being aware of what you are doing brings change of its own volition.

He was a Lord of the Realm, dignified, aristocratic, and imbued with noblesse oblige. He would have lunch at his club every day and then take a brisk constitutional. His assistant would tag along and he would issue instructions as they walked. Much business was usually accomplished.

He would pass a panhandler every day at the same corner and would drop ten shillings into his hat. That was a goodly sum in those days, but the recipient showed no gratitude. He was rude, ungracious, frequently inebriated. Sometimes he was even vituperative.

One day, when the tramp was even more disagreeable than usual, the assistant could not contain himself. "Your Lordship, why do you continue to give money to such an undeserving hobo?" he queried.

"What would you do if you were in my position?" the Lord queried back.

"I would tell him what he could do with himself," said the assistant with feeling.

"There was a time when I did that," assented the Lord. "But then I realized what I was doing. It is my nature to help those not as fortunate as myself. When I brushed him off in anger because of his surliness, I

was letting him dictate how I would behave. And I will not let a wine-sotted, foul-mouthed, unwashed vagrant decide my behavior."

The Witness will hold up a mirror and show you what you are really doing. And that knowledge produces change by itself. Sometimes it takes a while because you have built up a lot of momentum. Very frequently you lose the Witness. Find him every time you realize he has gone.

Do this persistently, and change *will* happen.

CHAPTER FIVE

You CAN Change
THE UNIVERSE!

⟖◦⟨⟞

My mother never went to college, but she was firmly plugged in to the wisdom of her tradition. She had developed a bedrock spirituality that she desperately wanted to pass on to me. She knew the Universe was a conscious entity. She was clear that material things come and go, but she had deep faith that the benevolence of the Universe would always permit one to surface even when engulfed by tidal waves.

I resisted my mother's wisdom like crazy. What did she know? She hadn't gone to college! These were dumb ideas. In fact, most of what she tried to teach me was contrary to everything I observed.

In India, there are many tales that mothers tell their children to inculcate my mother's kind of faith. Here is one such:

A traveler happened to come across a cherry tree that was right next to a watermelon field.

"How stupid of the Universe," he reflected. "Here is this stalwart tree

and it has such small fruit. And here is this huge fruit and it lolls around on the ground on a vine. It should be the other way around."

At that moment a cherry dropped on his head and bounced to the ground. He paused to think of what would have happened if that had been a watermelon.

And then he walked away marveling at the perfection of the Universe.

I had never heard of an M.B.A., but already that typical cynical questioning was an embedded part of my being. "Cherries don't hurt people and that's why they grow on trees, and watermelons can hurt people, so they grow on the ground, right?" I queried.

My mother nodded.

Then I delivered my one-two punch. "So how do you explain coconuts and durians?"

Coconuts on the tree are encased in a thick, green, fibrous, rock-hard casing. Durians are fruit contained within a hard shell with lots of tiny, razor-sharp spikes. Each weighs ten pounds or more. If either one drops on your head, you will not walk away pondering philosophical questions. In fact, you will not walk away at all.

My mother shook her head sadly but did not answer. I took her silence to mean that I had "won" and was mightily pleased with myself. I now know that she did have an answer, but realized that I was not ready to hear it. That was what made her sad. It was a long, long time before I was ready to understand.

What my mother was trying to tell me was that if one reaffirmed one's faith in the goodness of the Universe, it would act to protect one. "If a boulder was about to drop on your head," she would say, "faith will cause the Universe to change it to a pebble."

This did not sit well with me. It didn't make sense. It wasn't logical. I wanted to know why anything at all should drop on my head. I asked her to prove her contention. She couldn't. Whenever anything bad happened to her or our family, she would instantly note how it could have been so much worse and feel grateful that it wasn't. She tried offering this as "proof" that the Universe was busy converting boulders to pebbles, but I laughed so hard that she desisted. I wrote her off as a passive, misguided fatalist.

Years later, in college, I was playing squash with someone much better than I was. His boasts—the delicate shots that use the side and back walls to place the ball beyond the reach of an opponent—were exquisite and his expression was infuriatingly supercilious. I suspected that he avoided killing my loose returns simply so he could string me along and move me from side to side in a futile attempt to stay in the point. Soon, I could barely contain my rage.

Then, just as I was about to be shut out for the third consecutive game, I hit a perfect angle shot that caromed off the side wall and hit the front wall an inch above the telltale. Yet he got to it and looped his return high off the front wall and off to the side. Rushing to execute a put-away alley shot, I slipped on drops of sweat and careened into the wall headfirst, at full speed. My glasses broke and the steel frame dug into my face. I fell to the ground, unconscious.

It happened to be my birthday.

That afternoon I received a cheery letter from my mother calling down blessings on my head and expressing the hope that I was having a wonderful day. My reply was acerbic. No, I was not having a good day and how could she reconcile what had happened to me with the notion of a benevolent Universe?

She replied immediately, expressing gratitude that there was someone with me when I lost consciousness, someone who could take me for emergency treatment. She also pointed out how lucky I was that the steel shaft of my glasses, which could so easily have gouged out my eyeball, had merely inflicted a nasty flesh wound that would soon heal.

My reply was lacking in filial respect and would more appropriately have been written on asbestos. Fortunately, I had the good sense not to mail it. Instead, I shook my head at what I perceived to be her fantasy world. For the next two decades, I proceeded to live in a world where the Universe most definitely *did not* turn boulders into pebbles before they landed on my head. In my world, the Universe *threw* things at my head and its aim was unerringly accurate. It dispensed with cherries and pebbles and used coconuts and durians instead. When the stock of these ran low, it hurled watermelons and boulders.

It was not a fun place to be. But I believed in it completely. Are you, by any chance, living in this world, too?

PROOF CUTS BOTH WAYS!

My mother could not "prove" to me that faith in the benevolence of the Universe caused it to change dropping boulders into pebbles. What I failed to see, however, was that neither could I "prove" that it did not!

My mother's view and mine were at a stalemate, though I did not recognize that it was one. I spent years bashing my head against the granite walls of an uncaring and decidedly unbenevolent Universe before I started doing the exercises in this book. I started half-heartedly, but the results came so fast that I shook my head in disbelief and did them more seriously. And I discovered that another world did exist. It always had.

Back when I was young, even though I didn't realize it, I had a choice. I could live in a world where an intelligent entity worked to make life better for me and ameliorate the "slings and arrows of outrageous fortune." This was my mother's world. Or I could live in a world where random misfortune happened and I got more than my fair share of it. This was where I chose to dwell.

Between you and me, as a youth I made the wrong choice. My mother's Universe would have been ever so much better. But I guess I was still fortunate. I was able to cross over.

You don't need to have a revelation to make this change. You can do it now. I will explain how.

THE LAW OF INCREASE

Here is a mistake that most of us make. We believe that we are conscious, thinking entities, and if we think of it at all, we believe the Universe is a dumb, insentient mass. Indeed, sometimes it seems that the Universe consists solely of others who collaborate to consciously thwart us. At other times there is no malicious intent, there is just indifference to what *we* want. The net result is the same—we don't get what we would like to get. This is a common mental model that most of us have been using for a long time.

Try this mental model instead: The Universe is a conscious entity that is intimately intertwined with you and *not* separate from you. It *wants* to give you what you desire, and you *can* influence it.

The way in which you influence the Universe is simple and is summed up in the Law of Increase: *Whatever you are truly grateful for and appreciate will increase in your life.*

Skeptical? I don't blame you. Since I once felt the same way, I know that I can't change your mind. I am not even going to try to convince you. You will believe it only when you see it happening to you in your life, and that is exactly what the exercises at the end of this chapter will do. Bear with me till then.

What I am going to suggest is that you at least try to recognize that there are dozens of wonderful things in your life right now that you take for granted. They may include good health, a sharp mind, loving friends and relatives, and a lack of anxiety about where your next meal is coming from. Instead, what grabs most of your attention are the few things in your life that are not going the way you want them to, and you keep your focus obsessively on them.

Think of your life as two hungry dogs. The first is kind and gentle, the other disruptive and prone to violent attacks. You have a finite amount of food and can feed only one of the beasts. If you are like most of us, you will feed the demanding one, the one you want to pacify most. The one you are most afraid of. Now, which dog do you think will grow stronger?

That is the way most of us live. No wonder you feel "blah"!

Here is an exercise that will turn this dynamic on its head. In it, you will focus most of your attention on what is "right" in your life and almost totally ignore what is not. You will do what is necessary to fix or contain the bad stuff, but you WILL NOT expend emotional and psychic energy on it.

And you will wait for the Law of Increase to kick in.

Exercise: Appreciation and Gratitude Number 1

Try this for a week, for five to ten minutes every night, just before you retire. *It is important, so give it your utmost effort.*

Think of something that happened today for which you are thankful. Think of the numerous ways in which you are fortunate. Doubtless, you have many things to be grateful for. The fact that you don't have to give thought to where you will sleep tonight, the state of your health, your network of relationships, your mental faculties, the fact that you have the luxury of pondering the kinds of issues raised here, and much, much more.

Let a deep feeling of appreciation and gratitude well up in you. *Allow* this feeling to surface. *Permit* it to take hold of you, to envelop you. *Broadcast* it out as a silent statement of who you are. It is okay if you feel you are playacting. Do it with as much sincerity and emotional commitment as you can.

Think of as many things as you can for which you are grateful. *Remember: Whatever you are truly grateful for and appreciate will increase in your life.*

The timing of this exercise is important. This should be the last thing you do at night. Also, pay special attention to your "first thing in the morning" mental chatter the next day.

Exercise: Appreciation and Gratitude Number 2

After you incorporate the first part of this exercise into your life, try expanding it. Try letting feelings of gratitude take hold of you many times during the day. Don't force it. Introduce it gently and let it seize you if it can. If you can't, no harm done, but keep trying anyway. Observe what this does to your emotional tenor during the day.

You will find that it is easier to hold on to the feeling of gratitude if you use your body. Try walking with a spring in your step— even if you are simply rushing to the rest room during a seminar break. Smile, smile, smile. Don't smile with your face. Smile from your heart. Let laughter begin in the pit of your stomach, engulf you, and spread across your face.

When you interact with someone, even if it is a casual exchange such as paying a newsstand vendor for candy, earnestly wish that person every happiness possible. Do this silently. We do not want people with straitjackets taking you away! This may be a challenge for some of you if you have toxic people in your life. Do it anyway.

If you are hurrying somewhere and an acquaintance says, "Hi, how are you?" and you say, "Fine, how are you?" over your shoulder, slow down. Really look at the person to whom you are speaking. Observe the face, the expression, the body language. Wish him or her well silently. Sincerely.

It is perfectly okay for the transaction to be brief. Just be conscious and beam out peace and well-being as if your life depended on it. In a funny way, it does.

Specifically notice the following:

1. Do your feelings about people and the nature of your interactions change?

2. Do you perceive that others' feelings and interaction patterns have changed?

Finally, note what your emotional tenor has been during the week and how it compares to what it was earlier when you were doing the mind-chatter exercise and even earlier, before you started this book. Did you fall asleep more easily, and was your sleep deeper and more refreshing? What was your "first thing in the morning" mental chatter? Was it less insistent and more peaceful? Did you find yourself greeting the new day with more joy than before?

HELPFUL HINTS

Frequently, especially if you have had a tiring day, you may fall asleep as you try the gratitude and appreciation exercise. If this happens, try practicing it standing up or sitting up in bed. Then lie down afterward and go to sleep. If insomnia is an affliction for you, you will find that this exercise is a very powerful sedative. I cannot tell you how many people have reported that it has completely ended their difficulties in going to sleep. They also reported deeper, more peaceful slumber and feelings of peace and tranquility on waking.

If you find it difficult to beam health, prosperity, and other good thoughts to your rivals at work or to irritating colleagues, pause to consider their lives. Quite probably you have noticed that they carry around anger, frustration, envy, and similar emotional burdens. Imagine how terrible it must be to live like that. Feel compassion for their predicament and it is then a short step to wishing them well. Remember that you are wishing them well, but you are really doing this exercise for *you*.

You will soon see how this practice increases the good things in your life. It will not take long!

YOU CAN INFLUENCE THE UNIVERSE AND CREATE MIRACLES

Once you've realized that you can partner with the Universe through the Law of Increase, you will be more comfortable with the notion that you can influence the Universe, that you can cause miracles to happen. At first this idea seems so far-fetched that most of us don't even pause to consider it seriously. In fact, we spend a great deal of energy proving to ourselves that we cannot. We *know* that we are *not* God and that we cannot make miracles happen. We've reiterated this so many times to ourselves that we have convinced ourselves of our powerlessness.

Recognize this: For a miracle to occur in your life, it is not necessary to violate the laws of physics. It is not necessary to part the

Red Sea, as Moses did, or lift the mountain, like Krishna. For a miracle to occur in your life, all that is necessary is that you have the firm conviction that the Universe has intervened for you and on your behalf.

If you look sincerely for the miracles in your life, you will find them in droves and you will soon start producing them effortlessly. The problem is, because you dismiss this notion, most of the time you ensure that the exact opposite will happen. Let me explain how you do this.

Say you are driving to an important appointment and are running late. You are downtown at peak traffic time and parking is simply not available. Just as you arrive at your destination, a car pulls out of a choice parking spot right opposite the building you have to visit and you grab it. You don't even have to feed the parking meter because it has a lot of time left on it.

Do you congratulate yourself for producing another miracle? Of course not. You use a term custom-designed to annihilate any possibility of a miracle. You label it a "coincidence." You *know* beyond any possible doubt that you cannot produce miracles. You instantly recall the twenty-seven other times when you were in a similar situation and didn't find parking, and all the garages were full, and you couldn't even park illegally, in front of a fire hydrant, because even those spots were taken. So it has to be a "coincidence." And so it *becomes* one.

Now let's look at another scenario. You are starting to learn to play tennis and the coach has instructed you on how to hit a forehand. There is a ton of stuff you have to remember and do—take a deep backswing, bend your knees, hit the ball on the rise, catch the ball in front of you, begin your swing low and end high, push through the ball, end with your elbow facing your opponent, and on and on.

Your coach feeds you balls with the precision of a metronome and you swing away, but it does not go well. When you bend your knee, you forget to follow through, and when you try to push through the ball, you actually chop at it. Tennis balls form a parade of yellow blobs at the net and beyond the baseline and even in adjacent courts. You are frustrated.

Then suddenly something happens. Everything clicks somehow and you unleash a sizzling drive that goes low over the net and deep into the opposite court.

What do you do? Do you immediately disclaim responsibility and attribute it to "coincidence"? Or do you feel thrilled for a moment and then try to figure out what you did right so you can do it again? If you do the former, you will never learn to play tennis. You will probably do the latter and, in bits and pieces, eventually get your tennis game together.

These are examples of your mental models about the Universe at work. In the parking example, you *know* that you cannot produce those synchronistic happenings. But in the second model, the one that produces such wonderment and joy, you *know* that you can learn to play tennis. Look hard at these models. The first does not serve you well. But the second is transformative, powerful, and capable of delivering results.

Exercise: How to Create Miracles in Your Life

Have you ever had a wonderfully synchronous event happen in your life? Something that you would have classified as a minor miracle except that you know that "miracles don't happen?" Say you thought of a friend you had lost touch with and he called later that day. Say you were thinking of a quote and it suddenly showed up in a book or newspaper you were reading. Say you were wrestling with a problem and it was solved in a casual conversation that you overheard. Say you yearned for a particular type of candy and a friend mailed you a gift box that weekend.

There have been many, many such instances in your life. You decided to get back in touch with a classmate and found an e-mail from her waiting for you. You were trying to recall a favorite tune and the song was playing when you turned on the radio. You were dreading a visit from relatives and they decided to go on a vacation to some other part of the world.

Pay careful attention to such happenings. Explicitly recognize and acknowledge them. *Write them down!* List what happened, the date, and the time. Permit yourself to feel elated and write down this feeling as well.

Mentally, play around with the possibility that these were not "coincidences." That, somehow, a conscious Universe was trying to make itself known to you. Help it do so by paying close attention! Gently, very, very gently, try to make more such events happen. Try it in small ways at first. When you go shopping, *expect* to find that the item you want will be on sale. When you go bowling, expect that a particular ball—say the tenth—will be a strike. If you play tennis, expect that when the ad is against you, you will serve an ace.

Do this all the time. At least forty or fifty times a day.

There will be many, many times when you don't get the results you desire. Ignore them. Don't dwell on your disappointment. Acknowledge your mental chatter but simply let it pass. It is the equivalent of the forehands that you flub when learning to play tennis.

There will be a few occasions when you "succeed." Celebrate these. Jot them down. Allow the joy to envelop you when it happens. Allow the joy to come back and wash over you when you read about it in your notes and remember it. Remember, you are consciously using the Law of Increase. By celebrating these occasions, you are permitting more of them to appear in your life.

Gradually there will be a change in your thinking. As the number of instances multiplies, you will begin to wonder if they were really all "coincidences." You will begin to feel comfortable with the notion that maybe the Universe does work in the manner described. The moment this happens, you will notice that the number of such instances increases exponentially.

This is the signal for you to start to make bigger and more important things happen. They will indeed start happening, and you will struggle with "Omigosh! It really does work!" type feelings. Eventually these will dissipate and you will become comfortable with functioning in this manner as a regular part of your life.

Persist until this happens.

HELPFUL HINTS

Don't talk about producing miracles, or trying to produce them, with skeptical friends or relatives. Their skepticism can overwhelm you and make you feel both foolish and inadequate. Try it silently and let your own faith develop. Be patiently persistent. For some it may take a long time. That's okay just as long as you keep your intent alive and strong.

You *can* produce miracles in your life. You *can* engineer those amazing "coincidences" and lucky breaks that make life both invigorating and fulfilling. In fact, you can craft a life where a steady stream of such occurrences is "normal." Once you get used to doing this, you will wonder how you ever lived otherwise. Steve learned the lesson through a chance encounter. His story is below:

It was lunchtime when I finished my sales call and I was feeling pleased with myself. I had just closed a big deal and the client had given me a very warm referral and promised to call as well. As I waited for the elevator, two female executives came through the swing doors. I knew them both from innumerable meetings:

Eleanor was a good-looking redhead with an irrepressible smile. She had deep laugh dimples in both cheeks and seemed to have just emerged from a screening of a really funny movie. She was neatly dressed but, as usual, her clothes were rumpled. Joan was smiling now but, below that, frown lines were permanently etched on her face. As usual she was dressed impeccably.

They nodded pleasantly to me and the elevator arrived just at that moment. As we entered, Eleanor turned to Joan and remarked, "It's just past noon and I've already created my third miracle."

"What miracle?" asked Joan, puzzled.

"I'm in a rush today and have to get back to finish the new pitch book. So I made the elevator come right on time. Now I can just get to my favorite place and back rather than having to settle for a sandwich from that horrible deli." Eleanor was grinning and gushing. I sensed that she was egging Joan on.

"That's no miracle," snapped Joan. The smile vanished and a look of exasperation appeared. "Have you forgotten what happened two weeks ago?"

"Yes, I have. What happened two weeks ago?" queried Eleanor.

"We were supposed to have lunch together. You were in a rush again. Some moron was holding the elevator open on the floor above. These are smart elevators and the programming led them to believe that the nearby elevator would come for us, so all the other ones bypassed us. It was five minutes before the idiot released it, and when it came down, it was too full for us to get on. That's what happened," said Joan vengefully.

"I remember," agreed Eleanor. "It got so late that I had to skip lunch and go back to my office."

"Yes," said Joan, and her anger seemed to be building. "Where was your miracle-mongering then? There are eight elevators in this bank. This gentleman had already pressed the down button, so it was just chance that it came as we arrived." She nodded at me as she said this.

Eleanor nodded pensively.

"It's coincidence. Got that? Coincidence," said Joan emphatically. "Repeat after me: C-O-I-N-C-I-D-E-N-C-E. And, by the way, I'd be very careful what I say in front of others. Keep doing this and men in white suits will come to take you away."

The elevator reached the lobby and Joan strode away, her high heels click-clacking with emotion. Eleanor and I looked at each other and burst out laughing simultaneously. We understood each other perfectly.

"It must be terrible being Joan," I ventured.

"Yes," agreed Eleanor. "I wouldn't want to inhabit the world she lives in."

"But she did have a point," I prodded. "It wasn't a miracle any more than what happened two weeks ago was." I was curious to hear what she would say.

"Two weeks ago WAS a miracle," Eleanor responded. "It was an even bigger one. When I got back to my office, my phone was ringing. It was a headhunter I had known for years and he would not have left a message. One of his clients was about to make an offer to someone he thought was unsuitable. It was a completely different industry and he didn't think I would be interested, but he called me anyway, on a whim."

"And then?" I queried.

"We got along famously and I accepted the offer this week," Eleanor said, smiling. "I'm handing in my notice on Monday. There are too many toxic people in this place."

You do have a choice. You can be Eleanor or you can be Joan. Decide wisely.

TO CHANGE YOUR UNIVERSE, DISCARD THE MODEL OF "FRANTIC DOING"

Finally, I want to show you how you—yes, puny, insignificant you—can change your Universe. In fact, you've already proved to yourself that you can do it through the Law of Increase. But this method involves discarding the model of "frantic doing" that requires us, when we face a situation that we do not like, to DO something. Preferably *lots* of somethings. You have probably been using this model for most of your life. Not only that, but your parents, friends, advisors, and other well-wishers have probably been urging this on you. It is a completely accepted part of our culture and it crops up in countless sayings like, "The harder I work, the luckier I get." There are many examples in your life that contradict this model, but you have steadily ignored them. You don't even recognize them. Those experiences that validate this model grab your attention and seem to prove its veracity. This is a mistaken perception that most of us make as individuals and as societies.

Say we don't have a job and would like one. Frantic doing would have us send out dozens or hundreds of resumés, register with online job/career-related sites, make phone calls to potential employers or those who could lead us to potential employers, set up interviews, contact everyone in our network and try to tap into the networks of our network members, and so on. Simultaneously, this model would also require us to do things like make an inventory of our skills and talents and decide which we want to exercise. It demands that we decide on things like geographic preference, the size of the desired company, and industry preference. Then we target the universe of companies that meet these criteria and pray like crazy.

Say we are single and would like to be married, or at least in a relationship. This model would have us go out to bars or clubs or mixers; sign up with dating/matchmaking services; enlist friends and friends of friends to set us up with dates; join museums and book clubs and gymnasiums and other similar activity-oriented institutions; chat up attractive strangers on subways, in airport lounges, in restaurants, and wherever; go on blind dates; advertise in the personals sections; and do a ton of similar stuff. And, of course, we continue to pray like crazy.

This may work. It works often enough that you probably believe it is the only way to get what you want. The problem is that even when it "works," the results are frequently pretty poor. The job you find is actually one of indentured servitude. The relationship you get into has more than its fair share of aggravation. You've expended an enormous amount of energy, only to find yourself in a place that you don't really want to be in. You sink once more into that familiar feeling of being a gerbil in a cage, running on its wheel, getting nowhere. Quite possibly you feel that this is the "reality" of life.

It isn't. You *can* get off the wheel. Here's how.

When You Change, So Does the Universe

There is an alternative to "frantic doing." It is "calm being." Some of you will immediately recognize the truth of what I am presenting. Good for you. Go right ahead and start practicing it. Others will find the idea so strange and contradictory to what you have always believed that you will rebel. That's okay so long as you honestly try the exercises anyway. You will start believing when you see results showing up in your life.

Remember that the world you live in is not "the" reality. It is "a" reality that you have constructed. Each time you change one of your mental models, and do so at a very deep level, you become a different person. And when you become a different person, the Universe has no choice but to change in accordance with the person you have become.

Let me repeat that: *When you change, so does the Universe, and in conformity with your change.* It is as if you and the Universe are locked in an intimate dance, and when you lead in a different direction, it follows in lockstep. It cannot help but follow.

This means that in many cases you will be far more efficient in achieving something by doing "internal" work rather than by rushing around doing "external" work. Don't get me wrong. I am NOT saying that you don't need to do the external stuff. I am saying that there is much less of that needed than you think.

So if you would like a job, you need to free your mind from thoughts based on desperate want and instead concentrate on being crystal clear about what you would like. Enumerate what values are part of you and that your dream job would allow you to express. Become explicit about how it would benefit the larger society, and so on. When you are truly clear about this, the job flows into your life effortlessly, with very little action on your part.

If you are seeking a significant other, you can stop the ceaseless search and instead concentrate on becoming the person with the qualities of the one you would like to find. Once again, you will discover that the person you are seeking has appeared in your life.

If you feel that all this is "miraculous," you are right. It is. You can produce these miracles. When you become practiced in this way of being, you will be able to produce them almost at will. The biggest stumbling block in your way is your really deep-seated belief that you can do no such thing. This mental model is the concrete slab attached to your ankle that is pulling you down to the bottom of the ocean. Cut it loose and you will float effortlessly to the surface where there is lots of oxygen. You *can* cut it loose. You simply have to be patient. And persistent.

Am I advocating that you should stop "doing" the things you do to make something happen? No, not at all. Continue doing them, but even as you do, recognize that there is a better and more powerful way to bring about the change you are seeking. Try to use frantic doing and calm being in tandem. Gradually, experience will allow you to depend less on the former and more on the latter.

This is important because it generally takes a long time to learn to use "calm being" reliably. Not because it does not work, but because it is so contradictory to our views of "how things are" that we cannot bring ourselves to believe in it and accept it. We try to "experiment" with this new-fangled way, but we have strong doubts, and the Universe picks up on these reservations and reflects them back to us in the results it produces.

That's just the way it is. What you have to do is keep practicing the exercises in this book. Keep careful track of your "successes." Ignore your "failures."

Franz Kafka's quote below is very profound. It really gets at the essence of what we are talking about.

It is not necessary that you leave the house. Remain at your table and listen. Do not even listen, only wait. Do not even wait, be wholly still and alone. The world will present itself to you for its unmasking . . . in ecstasy it will writhe at your feet.

A NOTE OF CAUTION

If you accept what is presented in this chapter, it will permanently change the way in which you see the world. You will never again be the "victim" of forces beyond your control. You will team up with the Universe and cocreate the "reality" in which you live.

This is such a huge conceptual leap that you may be tempted to throw up your hands—and this book—with a sigh of despair. You may even feel that you have been "taken."

Don't do this! Try the exercises. Stick with them even if—as a result of your mental inertia—they don't seem to work at all. If you persist, you will eventually start getting results. Once you start seeing them, you will be more ready to accept them. They will appear faster and more plentifully, and before you know it, you will find yourself in an entirely new world.

I can tell you this from experience. I have seen innumerable people discover this for themselves. I cannot provide you with persistence. That you will have to supply from within yourself. Trust me when I say it will be well worth it.

CHAPTER SIX

Your "Me-Centered" Universe Creates the Stress in Your Life

——◆——

You live in a "me-centered" universe. We all do. Each of us evaluates events, near and distant, in terms of their impact on "me." If your spouse gets a great job offer, you think about how this will affect your relationship. When your daughter comes home with a tattoo and a nose ring, you think about how your friends will react and what they will think about your parenting. When you read about unrest in the Middle East, among other things you worry about the impact on oil prices and how much more you will have to pay for gas. You hear about a car accident on the radio and think in terms of how delayed you will be by the traffic jam.

Even your altruistic inclinations are frequently tainted. You want to do "good in the world" and to "give back" but it is important to you that you also be recognized for your actions. You want your jokes to be laughed at, your contributions to be acknowledged, and your advice to be solicited and acted upon. It is as if you walk through life with an invisible sign on your forehead: "This is ME. Pay attention. I am important." The sign may be invisible to others—even to yourself. But it's there nonetheless, informing many of your actions.

Susan was on the fast track—at least she thought she was. She had a relentless focus on her career and eschewed all activity that did not help her movement upward. She did not attend the Friday-night pizza parties unless she knew that her boss—or his boss—would be there. Then she would be the life of the party. She did not like volunteering, but chose to do so at the same disadvantaged-youth center the general manager went to. She even made sure she was there on the same days.

She turned down all requests for help, but was adroit enough to do so in a manner that showed she was really thinking of the company's best interest. "Sure I could do that, Bill, but I think that Ralph should handle it. He really knows the area and this is a great opportunity for him to demonstrate leadership. Let's nurture him along."

She always had a ready smile for everyone even though she had to really work at it because she disliked most of her colleagues. She cut down rivals, but was careful to do so with innuendo and misdirection rather than overt attacks. She always made it a point to direct honeyed words to persons she had maligned discreetly.

This was how big corporations functioned and she dutifully toed the line. Now it was time for her review. She expected to be made division head. The company had recently instituted a new evaluation process, but she was not worried. Had she not gone out of her way to be "nice" to everyone, at all levels?

The review was a shock—like walking unexpectedly into an ice-cold shower. "Insensitive," "Does not listen or pay attention," "Self-absorbed," "Not a team player"—the feedback shocked her. "But . . . But . . . that's not true," she protested weakly as she tried to make the case that she was none of those things.

"Yes, it is true, Susan," Jonathan, her supervisor, responded kindly.

"You go through the motions of compliance, but you are really out for yourself. You pretend to listen, but you are really trying to score points. People are not dummies. They sense this at a subliminal level. Everyone said something similar, so you really do have a problem.

"The good news is that they still like you because you do fine work. However, that will not last unless you can change your attitude. Let's talk about what you need to do. We need more time than I have now—how about next Monday at noon?"

You may think you are different from Susan, but let me show you how you are just like her. Go back and look at your mental chatter exercise and examine how often the word "I" comes in. "I" should have done this, said that, felt that. "I" am an idiot for doing this or not doing that. What will someone think of "me" for doing/saying something? How wonderful am "I" for pulling off that brilliant conversational riposte, that wonderful suggestion that others were too dumb to recognize the value of, that significant help "I" provided? Why can't "I" be as gorgeous as or as witty as or as brilliant as or as successful as or make as much money as X?

It is an unbroken and unending string of "I," "me," and "my."

Even when people are genuinely moved by compassion or love and sympathy, it does not take long for their "Is" and "mes" to creep back in. Tragedy in some part of the world? You call up the toll-free number in the news article to make a contribution, but it's amazing how swiftly your good intentions are followed by the thought, "How dare that person put 'me' on hold for so long?"

It's worth pausing for a few moments to think about this. Think about how *everything* you do is in some way a monument to "I" and "me."

Exercise: Me Me Me—O

This is a simple, on-the-spot exercise that you can perform at work. Get a small microrecorder or cassette recorder or activate the recorder on your computer. Make a business phone call where you have to convey an idea or sell a product to a client or coworker. Let the tape run and forget about it. When the call is done, play it back and count the number of times "I," "me," and "my" come up.

Don't beat yourself up about this. Just recognize and acknowledge it.

Also recognize, as Eliza Doolittle told Henry Higgins in *My Fair Lady*, that without your help, the Earth can spin, the tide comes in, the clouds roll by.

STRESS IN YOUR LIFE

There is always something happening in your home, your office, or the world. You observe whatever it is and react in terms of its impact on you. That's only natural. But it would be much more accurate to point out that what you really are reacting to is not the event itself but what you *think* its impact is going to be on you. And unless you can foretell the future, you, like most people, will find yourself frequently mistaken. Furthermore, you will find that the Universe has an unfortunate tendency of not paying any attention at all to what "you" want, and that is hard to accept. That lack of acceptance is the source of all the stress in your life.

This is a very important point—one worth pondering for a while. ALL of the stress in your life results directly from your fixed notion of how the Universe should behave and from your inability to accept the merry diversions that the Universe takes from your agenda. In fact, you generally take these departures from your script as a personal affront.

All of us want the people in our lives—spouses, parents, children, siblings, relatives, friends, neighbors, bosses, and coworkers—to behave in particular ways that we determine. We have specific—though often hidden—expectations for them all. We even want our pets to behave in expected ways. But they don't conform to what we want. Think of how much time and psychic energy you actually spend trying to "fix" these impossible people, to get them to behave in ways compatible with your notions. You try patient explanations, expostulations, outbursts of anger, pathetic pleading, threats and rewards, and whatever else you think might work. Yet none of them really do. Often, when you feel you aren't being heard, you crank up the volume on each one of these "requests" until they become a deafening roar in your head and in the heads of those around you. No wonder you feel such stress.

There are other ways in which the Universe does not cooperate with you. It rains when you are on vacation or have planned a golf outing. You expect a promotion and it goes to someone else. Your bonus is half what you expected, or even less. You should have been nominated "employee of the year" but get a pink slip instead. The subway is late when you are in a hurry. The ways are legion.

But while the ways in which you are frustrated are scintillatingly diverse, the way you react is always the same. You punish yourself by being uptight, anxious, irritable, and depressed. You punish those close to you by snapping at them, being emotionally withdrawn, not spending time with them, and being generally unhappy.

It's a toxic cocktail.

And we drink it on many days. Perhaps even every day.

It does not have to be this way!

I'M GOING TO GIVE UP HAVING EXPECTATIONS

Since unmet expectations are the cause of your problems, you might be tempted to give up on them. The idea is both tempting and powerful. If you don't have any expectations to begin with, then you cannot be disappointed and you thus escape frustration. You will be happy. Right? WRONG!

It is impossible for you not to have expectations. Even the simplest action you take comes with an expectation. If you scratch your nose, you expect that the itch will go away. If you are reading this book, you expect that you will be better able to cope with your life. If you pull an all-nighter at work, you expect that someone will recognize your contribution and dedication and reward you suitably. Every action has an expectation embedded in it somewhere.

The problem is not with having expectations. The problem is with what you do when your expectations are not met. How do you react when what you want does not happen?

Begin with the clear understanding that you do have some limited control over your actions. But you have virtually no control over the outcome. Some of the time the result of your action will be what you anticipated and desired. Much of the time it will not. Sometimes you will be mildly inconvenienced. On other occasions you will confront an unmitigated disaster.

Say that you have been very preoccupied with work for a while, so you pick up some flowers for your wife as an act of loving kindness. She may accept them graciously and your gesture may lead to a deep conversation and the strengthening of your relationship. Or she may blow up at what she perceives as your attempt to "buy" her affection and may accuse you of all kinds of malfeasance—from general thoughtlessness to infidelity—and before you know it, you find yourself in a full-fledged marital scrap.

Or you want to get closer to your teenage daughter, so you solicitously ask her what she is doing. She may respond animatedly or she may throw a tantrum at this unwarranted intrusion into her life. You exercise initiative at work and do something that is not a direct part of your responsibility. Your boss and peers may be highly supportive and make you feel good about having taken this extra step. Or you may get your knuckles sharply rapped for intruding on somebody else's turf and trying to usurp their authority.

The ways in which the Universe ignores our desired results are endless. You do something and expect outcome A. Sometimes you get it. And when you do, you pat yourself on the back for being such a smart manipulator of your destiny. But, more frequently, you get the unexpected outcomes B, C, D, E, and F. Think about it. Isn't this more usual?

The ONLY way you can prevent toxic feelings from being generated inside yourself is to accept whatever outcome actually occurs. It is better if you can cheerfully accept it. It is still better if you can embrace it. How to do this is explained below. Please note that "embracing" an outcome different from what you expected DOES NOT mean that you compromise your values or give in to your enemies. This is also explained below.

Good Thing, Bad Thing, Who Knows?

The first thing you do when you face an outcome different from what you expected is to judge it. You label it "good" or "bad," but generally "bad." The greater the deviation from what *you* wanted, the worse you think it is.

The following Sufi tale is instructive.

An old man lived in a verdant valley with his son, a handsome and dutiful youth. They lived an idyllic life despite a lack of material possessions and were very happy. So much so that feelings of envy arose in their neighbors.

The old man used practically all his savings to buy a young wild stallion. It was a beautiful creature and he planned to use it for breeding. The same night he bought it, it jumped over the paddock and disappeared into the wild. The neighbors came over and commiserated. "How terrible," they said.

"Good thing? Bad thing? Who knows?" said the old man.

Ten days later the stallion was back. It came with a herd of about a dozen wild horses, and the old man was able to lure all of them into his paddock, which he had fixed so escape was no longer possible. "What good fortune!" said the neighbors as they clustered around.

"Good thing? Bad thing? Who knows?" said the old man.

His son started to train the horses. One of them knocked him down and stomped on his leg. It healed crookedly and left him with a permanent limp. "Such misfortune," said the neighbors.

"Good thing? Bad thing? Who knows?" said the old man.

The next summer, the King declared war. Press gangs came to the village and rounded up all the young men. The old man's son was spared because of his game leg. "Truly are you lucky," exclaimed his neighbors as they bemoaned their own losses.

"Good thing? Bad thing? Who knows?" said the old man.

That very winter . . .

And that's the way it goes. This is highly relevant to you. Stop right now and think about it. Can you look at something that is bothering you in your life and see how it could be a good thing or a bad thing? Can you acknowledge that you just don't know?

Exercise: Good Thing? Bad Thing? Who Knows?

Look back on your life. Have there been any events that you classified as disasters, as totally terrible things, that you now recognize as true blessings? Pick something that you are still grappling with. Envision circumstances in which what you now see as a "bad thing" may actually be a "good thing," perhaps even a "wonderful thing."

There are strong elements of "If you get a lemon, make lemonade" in this exercise, but it actually goes deeper. I am inviting you to consider the model that you are NEVER given a lemon. You are given the opportunity to make lemonade. Even better, you are given the opportunity to make a double-dip sundae that tastes delicious and actually causes you to lose weight!

A NOTE OF CAUTION

Some of you may have had life experiences so painful that you cannot handle thinking of them as "good things." Examples are the death of loved ones, troubled relations with close relatives, serious injury, etc. Don't force yourself to work with such situations if you are not ready to. Pick something that you are comfortable working with. I will wager that there are enough "bad things" in your life that you can easily select one!

One of my students carried the trauma of a serious accident. She was almost completely paralyzed, in tremendous pain, and spent four years in a hospital flat on her back. While she does not classify her experience as a "good thing," she certainly recognizes its role in shaping her life and acknowledges that she received some very deep insights that are standing her in very good stead.

Finally, can you think of "good things" in your past that actually turned out to be "bad things"? DO NOT play this exercise in reverse. Accept the "good things" in your life at present as they are. Don't try to see how they could be "bad things."

SURRENDER TO THE UNIVERSE

When something happens in your life, you don't really know if it is a "good thing" or a "bad thing." If you look back, you will probably come up with quite a few instances where something that you initially thought was terrible actually turned out to be quite beneficial. I was once in a leadership position from which I was ousted by conspiratorial collaboration. It hurt my ego terribly. But looking back, I can now see that it also gave me the flexibility and time to develop a project in which I was passionately interested. This project eventually took off—and succeeded fabulously. In retrospect, what I thought of as a setback was certainly the best thing that could have happened to me. Even my ego needed that healthy pruning.

There are many such instances in your life. There are also many instances where you thought that something wonderful happened, and in fact it turned out to be quite crummy. Think of all the M.B.A.s hired by Enron in the weeks before it imploded who were congratulating themselves on landing offers with such a prestigious company.

This new perspective is important in eliminating the stress in your life. When you are less attached and sure of the efficacy and importance of certain outcomes, you are less emotionally bound to results beyond your control. Remember that the stress in your life is caused by your reaction to not getting what you want. Here's the good news: *You can eliminate all this stress by surrendering.* This is one of the most powerful concepts in this book. If you understand it thoroughly and succeed in implementing it in your life, more than 90 percent of the stress you are experiencing will simply disappear. Just like that. Poof! It will leave your life and the relief you feel will be palpable and immediate. Aladdin's genie could not produce a more satisfactory and complete outcome.

"Surrender?" you ask. "Isn't that a sign of weakness?" A sign that you've lost? Do you worry that if you surrender in a competition, your coworker will get the plum assignment or that you will never land the client you desire? Don't worry! You are not handing over your mind, your experience, or your creativity. You are not turning into a pushover. What you are surrendering is your agenda for what happens. What you are giving up are predetermined expectations. Because your stress is caused by your response to the results of your actions, when you surrender to the possibility that these outcomes can be either good or bad and that you just don't know, then you are actually stronger and freer to capitalize on what does occur.

The process of surrender has four steps. It is important that you do them all:

1. First, take all actions with a clear understanding of what you would like to have happen. Be unambiguous about what it is that you would like to accomplish as a result of them.

2. Consciously wish that all outcomes be beneficial *for all parties concerned.* This is important. Our competitive society trains us to think in terms of "winning" at the expense of others. It does *not* have to be so. Instead, actively and sincerely wish that there are no losers.

3. Recognize that your actions are simply one possible way of achieving the outcome you want. Remember that you

have a limited understanding of all the forces at play and from that limited viewpoint have selected your course of action as the "best."

4. Detach yourself from the outcome. Accept whatever outcome the Universe provides. Surrender to the Universe. It's better for you if you cheerfully accept whatever comes your way. If you actually welcome the results wholeheartedly, your perspective on them will be transformed.

Can you detach yourself from the outcome of your actions? Absolutely, you can. It is a skill—just like learning to ride a bicycle. Why don't you do it already? Because you never thought to do it and because you had no idea of the tremendous benefits that accrue from doing it.

In all likelihood this is the first time you have considered the idea that actions, expectations of outcomes, and reactions to those outcomes are not all inextricably linked. For most of your life you have functioned as if these came together in a single package. You want something, you do something else to get it, and you are elated if you succeed and depressed if you don't, and that's just the way it is. And as you grow older, you don't get it more often than you do, and that's also the way it is.

That isn't the way it is.

Your actions are within your control. Not entirely, but to a large extent. The outcomes are not. Reactions to the outcome are within your power—but only if you reach out and exert the control that you have. And this takes practice, repeated practice.

The following exercise will give you that practice.

Exercise: How to Act, How to Surrender

Think of something important in your life right now—something that you really want to have happen and for which you are ready to exert considerable effort. Why do you want this to happen?

Say you are striving for a promotion at work and there are three others vying for that position. Why do you want to be promoted? Is it for ego gratification, to be known as the winner? Or is it because you genuinely think you can do a better job than the others? Or both? Recognize that if ego gratification is the major component of your motivation, the Universe is unlikely to play ball with you. Even if you get what you want, you will pay a heavy price in terms of personal well-being, on many dimensions.

Whatever your reason or reasons, be honest and acknowledge them. Think of how others will be affected if you succeed. What about the other three candidates? What about the people who will now report to you? What about all the people you will be involved with as you take on new responsibilities—from your family to customers ten time zones away?

Mentally, and sincerely, wish them all the best. Wish for each what is perfect for him/her. Recognize that you do not know what this is or in what manner it may come about. One of the candidates, for example, may be disappointed at losing out but will then leave the firm for another and go on to great heights.

To the extent you can, make sure that what you are trying to accomplish is the best for all concerned in the complex trade-off of life. Wish that this, or *something better* for everyone, comes to fruition.

Then go right ahead and pursue the course you have charted. You may get what you wanted. Or you may not. If not, acknowledge what has happened and be open to the possibility that it was really the best thing that could have happened to you. In fact, accept this. Can you "prove" this to be so? Of course not. But can you "prove" this to be not so? Again, of course not. So you might as well live in the first reality. It may seem contrived and forced at first, but eventually you will habitually live there.

You are now at a new starting point and you repeat the whole process again. When you let go of anxiety about the outcome, you will be amazed by how frequently you accomplish what you set out to do and how much more effective you become. Prodigious feats that you would not even have dreamed you were capable of will become a regular and common occurrence.

Just try it.

> The true husbandman will cease from anxiety, as the squirrels manifest no concern whether the woods will bear chestnuts this year or not, and finish his labor with every day, relinquishing all claim to the produce of his fields, and sacrificing in his mind not only his first but last fruits also.
>
> —THOREAU

There is power in that quote if you contemplate it and let it seep into your consciousness. And when you constantly act in that manner, you will discover another marvelous result. You will enjoy what you are doing far more. When you let go of attachment to the outcome, you have more emotional energy to focus on your actions, and whatever you are doing will release that equanimity, that joy, back to you.

Once again, just try it.

HELPFUL HINTS

We tend to live in a zero-sum world where our gain is someone else's loss. If we win a poker hand, others lose. It permeates our thinking. It also need not be so. It is so only if this is the only model we are prepared to accept.

Start considering that a problem may be solved so that all parties are better off. Think of life as a linear programming-optimization function. And then it will start behaving in that way. You will notice that the more you sincerely wish others well and try to help them, the more succor you will receive from unexpected sources when you most need it and least expect it. Go ahead and discover this for yourself.

Surrender Is NOT Passive Acceptance

Remember that surrendering is not passive acceptance. It is not lying down and taking what comes. It is not bowing down to injustice or to despots. All of these are charges frequently made by persons who do not understand the concept.

Let's make it clear with an example.

You see something "wrong" at work; let's say it's persecution of the weak. You try to mobilize coworkers to protest against it. You fail. Miserably. You are even penalized. You know your boss now has it in for you and is waiting for the right opportunity and time to give you a shove out the door. So what does "acceptance" mean in a situation like this? Does it mean that you give up what you were trying to do and acquiesce in whatever is happening?

Not at all!

What I mean by "acceptance" is that you simply acknowledge what has happened and that it is not what you wanted or set out to do. Instead, try to see that the Universe has spoken clearly, saying, "This is not the way." This is troubling enough. *Do not* compound the results and make your situation worse by feeling angry, or hurt, or dejected. Try noting the outcome as dispassionately as you can—like a tennis umpire making a line call.

Once you have successfully detached yourself from an undesired result, let the experience become a new starting point for you. You can then go back and reevaluate your actions. You may well decide that what you should do next is repeat your actions, but this time with more intensity. Or you may decide that you need to rethink your tactics. Or your strategy. Or both. You may decide that you need more help and should seek an alliance. Or many alliances. Or any combination of all these. But you will be able to think much more clearly about the situation, because you will not have an emotional attachment to any particular outcome clouding your mind and interfering with your efficiency.

It bears repeating: Acceptance does not mean "giving up." It means you recognize that you did not achieve what you set out to do, and you do this without any kind of emotional trauma. You do it without beating yourself up, as you probably do right now.

When you do this, you will find that you become more effective—exponentially more effective—when you can keep your negative emotions out of the way. And you will also find that when you act in this way, you begin to accomplish what you set out to do more often than before.

With practice, it will soon seem as if the Universe is collaborating with you instead of thwarting you at every turn. And it is. It is as if the two of you are locked together in an elaborate tango. And you are. This knowledge is exhilarating beyond belief.

It may well take time before you see this happening routinely in your life. Possibly years or even decades. It does not matter. You will, quite quickly, see enough instances of this happening to gain the confidence that more of it can happen. Persist patiently. You cannot fail.

Exercise: The "Other-centered" Universe

For one week, you will live in an "other-centered" universe. This is an incredibly hard thing to do for lengthy periods, so I suggest that you pick two one-hour time slots each day. During your selected times, you will do all things for the sole benefit of the person with whom you interact. In conversation you will *not* think about the brilliant reply you will make. You will focus on what the person is saying and feeling and think *only* of how you can be of service to that person. If possible, be of service anonymously, or to strangers, thus taking "I" and "me" out of the picture entirely. Think of how you can be of service to people you know well, to people you barely know, to society at large.

Use judgment! Do not give the contents of your bank account to a panhandler. It is not clear that this is a helpful thing to do anyway.

Be creative! One person left gifts of candy for officemates, along with handwritten, anonymous notes expressing appreciation for some positive trait that person expressed. Another paid for tolls for the person behind him and gave the toll collector a page of uplifting quotes to give the person. Another person would—after she had finished with it—leave an unlimited day pass for the New York subway taped to the turnstile, along with a note saying, "This is an unlimited-ride MetroCard for today. It is meant for someone in need. If you think you qualify, please take it and use it. If there is still time after you are finished with it, please tape it to the turnstile from which you exit, with this note." Another would tape coupons for products she didn't need to the supermarket shelf where that product was stocked.

Each day, deliberately and consciously, do more than one thing to make the world a little better. The father of one of my son's friends is into the active life. Whenever he goes hiking he takes a large plastic bag and quietly retrieves discarded plastic bottles on the trails. Do you get irritated when you see a shopping cart ruining a supermarket parking spot? Get into the habit of taking one and returning it to the nest of carts at the entrance. Do you see a clearly misplaced sweater in a department store? Restore it to its rightful place.

The possibilities are endless. Spread sweetness and light. These are similar to "random acts of kindness" but, wherever possible, give specific help to specific people who need that help. Is someone you know having a hard time in a particular area of her life? Think of one thing you can do to make it a little easier for her. Even a card with a thoughtful quote in it may help.

Be practical and empathetic. A woman wanted to help a friend whose husband died suddenly, leaving her with small children. "What can I do to help?" was met with polite thanks. So she thought awhile and organized a group of friends. One went and gathered all the children's shoes and polished them for the funeral. Three others arranged to bring the family breakfast, lunch, and dinner for a week. Another woman contributed several hours of baby-sitting for the youngest child. None of this would have happened if the first friend had not set it up.

As you do this exercise, your attitude is important. If you help someone, *do not* expect gratitude from that person. Instead, *you* should be grateful to that person for providing the opportunity to be of service. Try it. This is a very different paradigm from the one we normally use. Don't resent people for not acknowledging how much you have helped them. Instead, keep your focus on being grateful for having had the opportunity to help.

Finally, each day, *make someone's day.*

The results of this practice will show up immediately. But

you have already experienced them without being conscious of it. Haven't you ever had a random interaction with someone that left you feeling so good, it uplifted your mood for an entire day? Perhaps it was a salesclerk who sincerely assured you that you looked really lovely in the dress you were trying on. And you somehow sensed that she cared about you and was not just out to clinch the sale. Perhaps it was the jovial guy in line next to you who cracked jokes that left you doubled up with laughter. Perhaps it was an unexpected and thoughtful gesture from a friend that really touched you.

This exercise means that you will go out, each day, and deliberately make someone's day brighter. Just the thought of having to do this will get your creative juices flowing. For some, it will also arouse fears. The shy will feel particularly pressured. Use this as a lever to overcome your shyness. Or else figure out how to do it anonymously. But DO IT. Do it at least once every day.

Eventually you will want to make this practice a part of your life, not an exercise to be completed. This is true of all of the exercises you are given in this book!

Helpful Hints

It is very common for people to try the "Other-centered Universe" exercise and be disappointed, even dejected, because the actions they took were not acknowledged or appreciated. If you find yourself traveling this road, stop immediately.

You are doing this exercise for *you*—not for someone else and not to get specific reactions from others. Focus on how you are feeling when you are doing what you set out to do. Eventually you will find your joy in what you do, not from the results you get. If you are appreciated and it feels good, that is a bonus. It is *not* the aim. You may feel awkward initially. Indeed, some might feel awkward for quite a while. But persist in the exercise.

It is also common for people to throw up their hands and say, "There is nothing I can do to make this person's day." This is intellectual laziness. Of course there is a lot you can do. Unleash your creativity. Get yourself a copy of a classic such as Alex Osborn's *Applied Imagination* and read it. Students in creative-writing classes are told to unlock the story in every humdrum person they meet—even the corner newspaper vendor. The story is always there. They just need the perspective and the ability to unlock it. This is equally true of you. There are ways. Just find them.

Be sure to write down the results of this exercise in your journal. Flip back through your earlier entries. You will be pleasantly surprised by how much your life has already changed and the progress you have made in creating an "alternate reality" for yourself.

Keep going. Now is no time to stop!!

CHAPTER SEVEN

FREEDOM AND HAPPINESS:
THEY AIN'T WHAT YOU THINK

—▶─◀—

"It's your wife," his administrative assistant said, handing Bryan the phone. "She says it's urgent."

"Are you going to miss Andrew's play again?" Her tone was accusing, but also resigned.

"I can't help it, honey." Bryan spoke in low tones. He moved to the corner of his office to get some privacy. It was a futile quest and he knew it. His office was crowded. The lawyers were at the round table. The investment bankers were camped out on the sofa and the accountants and bankers were huddled around his desk poring over stacks of printouts. He had a huge office and it was packed almost as tightly as a Manhattan subway at rush hour.

"United Manufacturing has just put in a hostile bid and they're two dollars above us," he continued. "I have to . . ." He stopped as he realized he was about to reveal secret information he was duty bound to keep confidential.

"I'll call you later," he whispered. "Please apologize to Andrew."

"Do it yourself," she snapped and slammed down the phone.

Andrew would graduate from high school at the end of the semester. He loved dramatics and this would be his last school play. He had a leading role this year. Sadly Bryan realized he had missed every play. The higher he rose in the company, the less control he seemed to have over his time. Not for the first time, he felt as shackled as any convict being taken to a maximum-security prison.

He shook his head and came back to the present. He had to prepare a response. Counteroffer or negotiation? He started evaluating the pros and cons of each.

Like Bryan in the tale above, we want to be free and we want to be happy. This is such a given that we don't even question whether we know what these terms mean. We also casually assume that we all have the same understanding. But as his story shows, it's not so simple.

FREEDOM

What comes to mind when I say the word "freedom"? The ability to speak, worship, and assemble without fear? The right to bear arms? The right to make up our own minds, choose our own mates, or chart our own paths? There are many layers to freedom, but almost all of us define it too narrowly. We tend to equate freedom with the elimination of restrictions on our behavior. In our relentless pursuit of this goal, we are willing to reorder society, smash traditions, and lift taboos. Western society enjoys unprecedented amounts of these freedoms. We prize such freedom so much that we are willing to live with some of its less desirable expressions—pornography, illegal drug use, and popular entertainment that continually pushes the boundaries of taste and propriety. We are marvelously adept at titillating our jaded senses.

But there is another type of "freedom" that we have not achieved and are not even pursuing. This is the freedom from the constant desire for "more." We are still prey to this ruthless feeling, which constantly spurs us into action, ignites avarice, and produces overweening ambition. This desire for continually increasing wealth and power too often goads us into activities that consume all of our available time and energy. We are driven by our demons, all of us— takeover titan and leveraged buyout artist, corporate chieftain and newly minted M.B.A., serial killer and confidence trickster, presidential candidate and overworked janitor. The talons of our addictions shred our minds and wreck repose. No, we don't think about freedom from these desires—the desires that become addictions. Sure, we recognize that some addictions—like to cocaine—are harmful, and we declare them illegal. But others, like workaholism, we applaud and reward.

Until we begin to think about freedom in a way that embraces our desires, like it or not, we will continue to be in the fierce grip of our restless minds, being blown hither and thither like a tumbleweed in a hurricane, expending our psychic energies in emotional roller coasters that we are helpless to stop and unable to leave. This, too, is a prison, and in our saner moments we want out. Oscar Wilde described this despair beautifully in "The Ballad of Reading Gaol."

> *I never saw a man who looked*
> *With such a wistful eye*
> *Upon that little tent of blue*
> *Which prisoners call the sky,*

And at every wandering cloud that trailed
Its raveled fleeces by.

We are surprisingly cavalier when it comes to giving away this critical form of freedom. Every time we imagine it will come from a better job, a different relationship, more money, or something else that is presently eluding us, what we are really doing is handing over to others the power to determine our happiness and tranquility. And most of the time we do not even recognize that we are doing so.

Stone Walls Do Not a Prison Make

There is a maelstrom in our mind, in every one of us. We have all felt its awesome power. At short notice, or no notice, it can plunge us into the whirling depths of watery despair. Reflect on how often this happens to you. Think back to the last time it happened. Is your company being taken over? Fear for your future is an icy hand upon your chest. Is your marriage shaky? The pangs of loneliness and desire for companionship are clammy and unwelcome companions. Does your mirror show sagging flesh and excess avoirdupois? There is increasing desperation in your oft broken resolves to eat right and exercise regularly.

Imagine a day when you got up in the morning and were well rested. You went to work and were pleasantly challenged. You labored intently but without a trace of anxiety. You felt no sense of frantic striving, no feeling of time running out and too much to do before it slipped away. When you returned home, you enjoyed the company of a good friend with whom you had a conversation that left you rejuvenated. There was no tension in the air, no sense of one-upmanship. If you watched television, it was a program that you really wanted to see, one that was instructive and elevating and that left you with an enhanced sense of possibility and a marvelous appreciation of the wonders of the universe. Finally, you went to bed, where you effortlessly drifted off to sleep cushioned by a deep sense of gratitude.

Do you even remember when you spent a day like this? If you do, rejoice wholeheartedly because you are assuredly not part of the multitudes. But if you want a lifetime of days like this, it is crucial to escape from the prison of your uncontrolled desires. You will truly become free.

Uncontrolled? You don't think of yourself in those terms. But before you scoff, try this simple exercise that will reveal how out of control your life truly is.

Exercise: Doing Nothing

Find an easy chair and sit down comfortably. Set your alarm clock to buzz in a half hour. For the next thirty minutes, you will DO NOTHING.

By that I mean no watching TV, reading newspapers or magazines, checking e-mail, or scurrying around doing chores. No drifting off into a sexual fantasy or a Walter Mitty–type daydreaming scenario. Just sit and be aware of your surroundings. If you wish, you may pick an item—a photo on the side table, the texture of the carpet, a tree outside the window—and contemplate it. That's all.

You have done the mental-chatter exercise, so you have some idea of the beasts you harbor inside you. You will still be bowled over, however, by the ferocity of the forces you unleash with this simple act. You will experience deep unrest and agitated feelings that you are "wasting time" and should not be doing so. The inability to concentrate on whatever you select will combine with these anxieties and build a feeling of intolerable pressure. That half hour will seem interminable. You might not even be able to make it for the full time of the exercise.

If you are unable to spend a quiet half hour by yourself, how "free" do you think you really are? Think of your life right now. Are you driven by irresistible urges—for food, for drink, for cigarettes or drugs, for unwholesome entertainment, for tawdry thrills? Do you reach for the TV remote not because there is something you really want to watch but because you need to beguile the restless monkey that is your mind? Do you ever find yourself doing things that you know you should not but you do them anyway? Envying people you don't even like? Talking about them behind their backs? Are you really free if you cannot stop yourself from taking actions you don't want to take? No, if you are like most of us, you are not free from these almost involuntary behaviors. You are in a prison of your own making, battered mercilessly by the conditioning you have been subjected to and the mental models you have constructed from them. Models that you resolutely refuse to abandon. You reach the same recognition as the poet Richard Lovelace.

> *Stone walls do not a prison make,*
> *Nor iron bars a cage;*
> *Minds innocent and quiet take*
> *That for an hermitage.*

Do you have an innocent and quiet mind?

To be truly free, we have to expand our notion of freedom. We have to move beyond thinking that it results from not having someone or something dictate what we should do or how we should think. That is an essential freedom, but it is not the only one. The ability to actually do what you recognize is in your best

interests—in your calmer, rational moments—is equally important. We focus altogether too much on the former and don't even
acknowledge the latter.

It is this second facet of freedom, the one we ignore, that is the
key to lasting happiness. Bryan, in the opening story, was so fixated
on career success and moving ahead that he did not even realize he
was completely surrendering his life. When he did, it was too late.
He was trapped in a prison that he had created himself.

HAPPINESS

We seek it here, we seek it there, we've learned to seek it everywhere, like Frenchmen looking for the Scarlet Pimpernel. And yet
this chimera eludes us with the facile grace of a gazelle disappearing in craggy mountain heights. All of our activities—our pursuit
of fame and fortune, our quest for meaningful relationships, our
drive to build or change things—are directed searches for this
ephemeral state. We get there, but we can never heave a lasting sigh
of relief because we leave before we are ready to.

What is "happiness"? Can it be a permanent member of our
household rather than an itinerant visitor, like the title character
in Rabindranath Tagore's *Kabuliwallah*? Below is an exercise developed by the psychotherapist and Jesuit priest Anthony
DeMello:

> Recall the kind of feeling you have when someone
> praises you, when you are approved, accepted, applauded.
> And contrast that with the kind of feeling that arises
> within you when you look at the sunset or a sunrise, or
> Nature in general or when you read a book or watch a
> movie that you thoroughly enjoy. Get a taste of this feel-

ing and contrast it with the first, namely, the one that was generated within you when you were praised.

Understand that the first type of feeling comes from self-glorification, self-promotion. It is a worldly feeling. The second comes from self-fulfillment. It is a soul feeling. Here is another contrast: Recall the kind of feeling you have when you succeed, when you have made it, when you get to the top, when you win a game or bet or argument. And contrast it with the kind of feeling you get when you really enjoy the job you are doing, you are absorbed in the action you are currently engaged in. And once again notice the qualitative difference between the worldly feeling and the soul feeling.

Yet another contrast: Remember what you felt like when you had power, you were the boss, people looked up to you, took orders from you; or when you were popular. And contrast that worldly feeling with the feeling of intimacy, companionship—the times you thoroughly enjoyed yourself in the company of a friend or with a group in which there was fun and laughter. Having done this, attempt to understand the true nature of worldly feelings, namely, the feelings of self-promotion, self-glorification. They are not natural, they were invented by your society to make you productive and to make you controllable. These feelings do not produce the nourishment and happiness that is produced when one contemplates Nature or enjoys the company of one's friends or one's work. They were meant to produce thrills, excitement and emptiness.

Then observe yourself over the course of a day or a week and think how many actions of yours are performed, how many activities engaged in that are uncontaminated by the desires for these thrills, these excitements that only produce emptiness, the desire for attention, approval, fame, popularity, success or power. And take a look at the people around you. Is there a single one of them who has not become addicted to these worldly feelings? A single one who is not controlled by them, hungers for them, spends every minute of his/her waking life consciously or unconsciously seeking them? When you see this you will understand how people attempt to gain the world and, in the process, lose their soul.

And here is a parable of life for you to ponder on: A group of tourists sit in a bus that is passing through gorgeously beautiful country; lakes and mountains and green fields and rivers. But the shades of the bus are pulled down. They do not have the slightest idea of what lies beyond the windows of the bus. And all the time of their journey is spent in squabbling over who will have the seat of honor in the bus, who will be applauded, who will be well considered. And so they remain till the journey's end.

Too many of us are like these tourists, engaged in petty power struggles while the true beauty of life lies all around us, unobserved and unappreciated. I see this all the time in the seminars I conduct when I have participants list the things that would make them happy. That list grows fast, and fifty to a hundred items come on the flip chart in minutes. Wealth is very common. Not run-of-the-mill, garden-variety wealth but a fabulous fortune. The kind of wealth that gives you mansions where you need a golf cart to get to the dining room. A trophy spouse is another popular item, though people rarely label one as such. Instead the desired spouse will be described as someone who is first extraordinarily good-looking and, as a self-justifying afterthought, intelligent to boot.

Lots of other items come up, such as travel, good health, great sex, fame, power, friends, loving relatives, and interesting work. Many say having the resources, time, and talent for their special interests, such as vintage wine, rare art, the martial arts, would make them happy. Every once in a while, some people remember to list inner characteristics, such as faith or spiritual development, but these don't show up too frequently.

There is a palpable sense of shock when I take a huge red marker and slash it across that list and tell them that *none* of these things is necessary for happiness. *None* of them. Even the inner characteristics mentioned above won't create happiness, although they do appear spontaneously as by-products. But they are *not* prerequisites.

Think about this for a while. It is an extremely important point. If anything that you can *get* through external sources will give you happiness, then isn't that an extremely frail reed to lean on? Do you really want to spend your whole life in the quest for something so dependent on outside circumstances that are never going to be in your control?

Whenever your inner emotional state is dependent on something external, you can *lose* whatever you *get.* Do you really want your happiness to be based on such fickle foundations? A senior executive spent years angling for the top job. He cultivated superiors, went out of his way not to antagonize any peer or influential subordinate, carefully built up his resumé with showcase successes in different operating divisions, and buried his failures with great care. He played the corporate game to the hilt and heaved a huge sigh of relief when the directors finally offered him the CEO position. It had taken him more than twenty years to get what he had sought. Less than forty-eight hours after taking the reins, his largest competitor launched a hostile takeover and quickly sewed up a majority of outstanding shares. The executive had not yet signed his new CEO contract and was out of the company with no notice.

When you lose whatever you have gotten, does your happiness vanish with it? Does it have to be that way? The answer is absolutely not. Your happiness is *not* dependent on your wealth, your intelligence, or your other abilities. Your happiness is not even contingent on your continued good health, or your having loving friends, relatives, or significant others.

In fact, happiness is already a part of your innate nature. There is *nothing* you have to do or get in order to be happy. All you have to do is allow it to surface.

When I get to this point in my seminars, I generally have a revolution on my hands. There is vociferous disagreement. How can one be happy if one is extremely destitute? Or if one is in the grip of debilitating and painful disease? Or if one is unfortunate enough to be in the prison of a brutal dictator? Or if one has no friends or loved ones? And there are many, many more hypothetical scenarios posed, each designed to refute the statement made above.

Yet the statement holds. There is nothing you have to *get* in order to be happy.

Go back and read DeMello's eloquent thoughts about happiness again. Think about whether you have confused the quiet, unalloyed joy that he refers to as a "soul feeling" with the temporary feelings of satisfaction that come as a result of gratifying our egos.

THE POWERFUL BRAINWASHING

When the tumult dies down, one question remains hanging. If happiness is our innate nature, why do we not experience it more often? Why are our lives so filled with angst and sorrow?

The answer is simple: We have constructed mental models in

which happiness comes as a result of our getting something—money, power, spouse, children, fame, etc. In this reality that we have made and that we live in, our achievements define us. We are "better" if we are "successful," and we buy into this with every fiber of our being. And we remain thirsty, like Tantalus, because the water never quite reaches our lips.

We have a great deal of help in these beliefs. The media subtly paints our pictures of what successful and happy people look like. In a delightful documentary entitled *Advertising and the End of the World,* Professor Sut Jhally of the University of Massachusetts shows how advertising has colonized our culture and usurped our values. Each of us is bombarded with more than three thousand commercial impressions each day. All of these carry the same subliminal message: "You are incomplete . . . your life is incomplete. What you need to make it complete is X." They are designed to make us feel unfulfilled, unhappy, and unsuccessful in order to create a desire for the products being sold as solutions to our manufactured needs.

I would be wealthy indeed if I had a nickel for every person who assured me that he/she was not influenced by advertising, that he/she simply ignored the flood of messages. This is partially true. We do resist purchasing many—even most—of the products that are pitched to us because of economic considerations and personal taste. What we don't understand is that even as we exercise prudent judgment in this area, we have already bought into the myth that stuff will bring us happiness.

Go back and look at the commercials during your favorite TV program. Look at the real, human feelings and desires that are portrayed so effectively—the camaraderie in beer advertisements, the sensual pleasure in shampoo commercials, the sense of relaxation in travel spots. And each of these is silently suggesting that the way to achieve that feeling is by consuming the product. We may not buy the suggested product, but we accept the dangerous premise that consumption provides happiness. And we shop till we drop.

Look at your life and your patterns of consumption. You are absolutely convinced that you need to maintain your particular "standard of living" and maybe even improve it a bit. Or a lot. You believe that doing so will free you from a situation where you are stuck and that happiness will result. You buy a diet aid and you will be free from fat and therefore happy. You buy a new golf driver that will free you from your pathetic tendency to shank the ball and you will be happy. Go right ahead. Try it. More power to you. The trap is not there. The trap is in the *belief* that if you succeed, you will be happier. Your purchases may or may not make you happier, but whether or not they do is beside the point. What matters is that we are so invested in the *idea* that external goods can make us happy that we do not even begin to recognize this. We have swallowed the insidious lies of the advertising establishment hook, line, and sinker. And this swallowing happened because we were not paying attention. Because we were so convinced we were immune that we did not even think of putting up our guard.

Relentless consumption is great for the economy. It may not be so great for you personally.

But advertising is only one facet of our brainwashing. There are innumerable other elements that have contributed to this deeply instilled belief in your head that you need certain things to be happy—wealth, health, beauty, fame, reputation, power, success, etc. Your parents, in subtle and not so subtle ways, reinforced this view and imprinted on your mind that what they found valuable was what you, too, should value. In all probability they got their beliefs from their own parents and accepted them equally unquestioningly. Your relatives, friends, teachers, classmates, and coaches all played a role. So did the movies and TV programs you watched, the books and magazines you read, the music you listened to, and what you observed in the world around you.

They all contributed. But they succeeded because you did not question the mental models being presented to you. But now, in your quest for happiness and freedom, you find you must question these beliefs, these values, these mental models, and the answers you will find are very counterintuitive.

IT'S OKAY THAT THE TREE IS CROOKED

In the previous chapter you learned that ALL of the stress in your life is caused by your inability to accept what the Universe is giving you. You have fixed notions of how things should be—how your friends should treat you, how your boss should view your suggestions, how your significant other should respond to you, even how vigorously your dog should wag its tail when you come home.

You saw that when these expectations are not fulfilled, too often your response is to become anxious, angry, depressed, weary, listless, frustrated, or some combination of these. Your weariness comes from trying to fix it so that the Universe conforms to your rigid notions.

You have discovered you cannot command the Universe to comply with your wishes. But what happens when it gives you something unbidden? Have you ever been confronted with a scene of such spectacular beauty that you were awestruck? The view from a mountaintop perhaps, or a verdant valley or a rock formation or a rainbow over the ocean while you were on a cruise. Can you recall the deep feeling of serenity and peace that enveloped you? Most people can, and that is one reason travel to scenic locations is such a prized vacation activity.

You have experienced the feeling, but have you ever wondered why it came to you?

That feeling of peace, that deeply nourishing experience happened because you—at that instant—fully accepted the Universe as it is. You didn't think, "If that boulder were a hundred feet to the left it would be so much prettier" or "That tree is crooked. I need to do something about it" or "How nice it would be if the rainbow wasn't partially obscured by the clouds."

Oh, no! You accepted the boulder where it was and the partially visible rainbow was still magnificent and the tree was perfect in its crookedness. In fact, there was a rare beauty inherent in its very crookedness that you readily appreciated.

Your life is equally wonderful if you look at it dispassionately, as an admiring spectator. But you don't. If you are a politician, you look at people in terms of whether they are for you or against you or what they can do to help you get elected. If you are desperately single, you look at people as potential mates, or as someone who could introduce you to one, or as irrelevant. *You never see the world as it is, you see it as you are.*

We are always clinging, and what we are clinging to keeps changing. We have a wonderful time with good friends at a great restaurant, so we keep trying to re-create it. We get recognition at work, like it, and try to get more. There is a note that plays all the time in our heads: "This is good. May I have more of it. May it never end." And, of course, we flip it when we are confronted with stuff we don't like. We go: "This is terrible. May it end immediately. May I never have to undergo this again." Remember that aversion is also a form of clinging. You are clinging to the absence of something.

Anytime we want something, and we get it, there is a brief moment when we are content, when we are not our habitual wanting self. And in that moment we experience the happiness that is always a part of us. We are content. And full. But the very next moment, some other desire raises its ugly head and we are off on our fruitless quest again. It is a never-ending cycle.

The problem is that we do not recognize that the happiness we experience is because, at that moment, we are free from want. It springs from an acceptance of the Universe as it is. It is simply our innate nature bubbling forth in the absence of the constraints we put on it with our incessant demands.

Instead, we ascribe the happiness we briefly felt to the acquisition of whatever it was that we got. And so we try to get the next thing, and the next thing, and the next thing. The story below says it all:

> *The acolyte prostrated himself before the Master. "Holy Sir, I have spent six years in your service. You promised me that you would tell me the secret of enlightenment on this anniversary. Please do so now, for I am weary of this pointless existence."*
>
> *The Master looked fondly at his disciple. "Yes, it is time," he agreed. "You will become enlightened when you stop being like that dog," he said, pointing at an emaciated mutt that was trotting by.*
>
> *The disciple looked at the dog. It was starving and had open sores. Its ribs stuck out and it was desperate in its demeanor. "How am I like that dog?" he queried, puzzled.*
>
> *The Master said nothing, but followed the animal. The disciple kept pace with him. By and by the dog spied a dry bone and pounced on it. The bone had jagged edges and sharply cut its tongue and mouth and the blood flowed. The dog licked its chops and chewed harder.*
>
> *"The blood and flesh it is tasting are its own," said the Master, "but the dog thinks it is from the bone. And it keeps chewing the bone even though it hurts itself more the longer it does so."*
>
> *"So?" said the disciple.*
>
> *"The peace, contentment, and joy you seek are inside you," said the*

Master. *"But you keep hunting for it outside. The worldly things you pine for so desperately and collect so avariciously wound you in the same manner the bone cuts the dog, but you think the pleasure you derive is from those objects and cling to them more ferociously."*

The disciple stood dumbstruck. The picture was uncomfortably vivid. Blood was dripping from the dog's mouth and staining the road, and still the dog bit at the bone with apparent relish. He looked at his own life of striving, and the parallel was painfully clear.

"My son," said the Master with great compassion, "you can only truly enjoy the things of this world when you do not cling to them and when you do not ascribe your happiness to them. Just try this and see for yourself."

MAKE CHANGES, BY ALL MEANS

So what does "acceptance" mean? Does it mean that you don't try to change whatever you see as wrong? If your boss is abusive, do you roll over and "take it"? If politicians propose policies you consider ruinous, do you acquiesce? If entrenched power and privilege move against you, do you lie down?

Absolutely *not*! In fact, you fight the good fight with every fiber of your being. But you fight it with the knowledge that this is your path in life, that your motivation is to bring about an outcome that is better and beneficial for all parties involved. Act with the full acceptance that what you do is somewhat within your control, but the results are not. Uncouple your well-being from the upshot and calmly, even gratefully, accept whatever happens, even if the outcome is something you view as disastrous. This *can* be done. It is a learnable skill.

If the outcome is terrible, take stock and look at the situation as an opportunity to make a new beginning. You can then decide whether to do what you did before with more vigor, or to do something different. But accept the results with the same equanimity for all of your actions and all of your life.

Here is the paradox: When you are *not* emotionally involved in a particular result, you are far more effective in bringing it about. There are countless examples from the world of sports. Tennis players have their service broken when they are serving for the match and think about how important it is to win. Golfers shoot double bogeys on the eighteenth hole when they let thoughts of winning grab them. Great players have an uncanny ability to focus on one point at a time, on one stroke at a time. They exult *after* the competition is over.

IT WILL COME IF YOU DON'T SEEK IT

If you go barreling through life in a full-throated charge, desperately doing things to make you "happy," happiness will elude you. It is like a puppy that runs away when you seek to entice it to come to you. Forget about making overtures and start reading your newspaper, and you will feel its cold nose in your hand.

He was a powerful monarch and presided over a prosperous kingdom. Art and science flourished and there was literature and theater and wholesome entertainment. His ministers were wise and dedicated. His wives were many and beauteous. His offspring were brilliant and dutiful. His army was powerful enough to keep all enemies at bay. He had leisure enough to pursue any field of learning and a mind keen enough to make rapid progress. There was nothing of this world he did not have.

Yet he knew that there was something missing. Serenity eluded him and his sleep was troubled. He eagerly sought out wise men who could possibly cure his malaise. One day he learned of a Sage in a distant town, a man of the greatest wisdom and accomplishment. He hurried thither to meet him.

The Mystic was emaciated and unwashed. His locks were unkempt and he was barely clothed. But his eyes shone with an unnatural light and the King somehow knew that he was in the presence of greatness.

"Tell me, sir," asked the King anxiously, "are you truly happy?"

"Of course I am, my son," he replied. "How could I not be?"

And the King knew it was true and he earnestly asked for instruction.

The Sage agreed, but the conditions he set were severe. For ten years he was to have the rule of the kingdom and the palace. If his slightest action was questioned, he would leave immediately. The King agreed and the Sage took up his abode in the palace.

He immediately started living a life of unbridled indulgence and luxury. Barbers and masseuses tended to him, the finest tailors clothed him, jugglers and clowns entertained him, and he had sculptors create massive statues of himself all over the kingdom.

The King was taken aback by this transformation, but he kept his word and instructed his staff to obey the Sage. They grumbled loudly and felt that the King had taken leave of his senses, but grudgingly they obeyed.

Every evening, for one hour, the King received instruction and the Sage seemed different at these sessions. His words carried the ring of truth and the ruler learned much about statecraft and about philosophy.

At other times he despaired and regretted his impulsive invitation. The intruder discovered tobacco and puffed like a chimney. He was introduced to intoxicants and imbibed freely. He made boundless use of the ruler's harem and the King shuddered and turned his head.

The breaking point came some months later when the King was with his favorite concubine and the Sage asked him to be gone so that he could indulge himself. Red-faced with wrath the sovereign berated him and asked him to look at what he had become, how low he had fallen.

"There is no difference between you and me," he asserted. "How could I have possibly thought that you had anything to teach me?"

"I was wondering when you would erupt," said the Sage in amusement. "I will leave now because you broke your word. You are wrong. There is an enormous difference between us and until you understand this difference, you will suffer as you always have."

"What difference?" the King shouted. "You indulge yourself just as I do and seek enjoyment more than I ever did."

"Your word was weak," said the philosopher calmly, "so I will leave. But you are a good man and your intentions were honorable, so I will teach you this difference as a parting gift. But I cannot do it here at the palace. You must come with me alone, for two weeks."

So the two set out and traveled far and the King kept pressing for answers and the Sage smiled enigmatically. At length they reached the border and the Mystic kept going. The King stopped even though the other pressed him to follow.

"It is not safe," protested the King. "I have to hurry back. There are affairs of state to tend to and much to do. I regret that I indulged you again. Tell me the difference and be gone."

"That is the difference, my son," said the Sage as he discarded his raiment. "I was in the lap of luxury and I leave with no regrets, not a moment's sorrow. The time for such enjoyment is past. Like all things, it comes and it goes and I accept this fully, with total equanimity.

"You, on the other hand," he continued, "are so stuck with being a King that you are prepared to forgo your own quest. This is the tragedy. What you seek is within your grasp, but you can only reach it if you let go of what you are clasping so tightly to your bosom. I understand this. You do not. That is the difference between us and it is a mighty chasm.

"Return to your palace. Rule wisely, my son, and I pray that some day you, too, will discover this truth for yourself."

The scales fell from the King's eyes and he remembered their evening sessions and how much he had learned. He earnestly begged for forgiveness and entreated the other to return.

"No, my son," said the Sage firmly. "If I return now you will forever doubt whether I was a master gamesman or a true Master. There is nothing more I have to teach you. Go back to your kingdom."

He turned and strode off. He did not look back.

The King returned to his palace and resumed his rule. He pondered the Sage's words and reflected on his teachings. And suddenly, one day, he understood.

It really does work that way. You are bound by the things you own as long as you need them emotionally. The moment you sever this psychological link, you will experience a marvelous freedom, a sense of liberation that cannot be described.

There is a story about Thomas Edison watching as his laboratory was engulfed in flames, his life's work disappearing in the blaze. He sent his son to summon his wife, because he did not think it likely that she would ever again see so glorious a spectacle. And the next day he began to reconstruct it.

Be like that and the world will be your oyster!

Exercise: List Your Accomplishments

Go over your life from your earliest memories and make a list of your accomplishments. Do this year by year until you were about ten, and then quarter by quarter until about two years ago, and then month by month until you come to the present. Use whatever you have available to jog your memory: diaries or journals; old photo albums; letters; appointment books. If you feel comfortable doing so, talk to parents, siblings, friends, relatives, or others who knew you at various stages of your life.

Write down everything you can recall that was memorable. It could be something others consider "trivial," such as a kindergarten teacher commenting favorably on your crayon drawing. It might be what others consider "important," such as landing a prestigious job. What is important is that it made YOU come alive and gave you a glow. It's perfectly okay if this is something no one ever knew about, such as the time you spent hours building a model that you never showed anyone. Re-create that feeling in your mind to the extent possible. What was satisfying about it? Have your own views on this changed over time?

After you have done this exercise, reflect on whether there are any patterns that pop up in the occasions you have recorded. For example, do you find that what gives you satisfaction is almost always related to helping others in some way? Or do you find that the moments you remember are when you were the center of applause?

How many of the items in your list are times when you were honest and authentic and being yourself? And how many are times when your ego was being stroked by others congratulating you and telling you how good you were? How many items evoked "worldly feelings," such as approbation? How many evoked "soul feelings," such as reveling in good company or excitement at some vista of knowledge?

What does what you find tell you about yourself?

This exercise will give you some idea of the extent to which you are dependent on others for your well-being. If most of the incidents you recorded are memorable because of the reactions of others—family, friends, peers, etc., then you know that you are in prison even if you cannot see the bars.

Exercise: Corollary

Think about some activity that you really and truly enjoy. Some activity that brings you joy. Something where it is totally immaterial to you whether or not anyone knows about it or how good you are by someone else's standards. It could be playing a musical instrument you always wanted to. Or writing a novel. Or painting or sculpture or card tricks or long walks. It could be reading nineteenth-century Russian fiction, or romantic poetry. Or developing your own photographs as you disdain digital formats, or inventing new board games, or making flower arrangements, or training dogs to do Pilates.

Whatever.

When was the last time you indulged in this activity? Set aside some time each week and indulge in it wholeheartedly.

Start immediately! DO IT NOW!

And as you do this, you begin honoring yourself. Acknowledge the calm joy you feel as you are immersed in this activity. Appreciate it. Be grateful for it. Give thanks to the Universe for allowing you to do this. By the Law of Increase more things will start appearing and happening in your life that will give you the same feeling.

Exercise: Dropping Destructive Habits

Do you find yourself prey to self-destructive behaviors? Do you explode in inappropriate anger? Are you addicted to smoking, or drinking, or controlled substances? Are you controlled by sexual thoughts or obsessed with persons or things?

Here is something that will help.

1. Clearly and dispassionately note the damage being done by your behavior. Recognize that you are NOT your

behavior. Don't beat yourself up about it. Just acknowledge that you have some bad habits and call it that.

Be aware when these behaviors are triggered. The mental-chatter exercise you have done is very good preparation for this. Timing is crucial. You should have this awareness the instant BEFORE you blow up, or drift into sexual fantasy, or reach for a cigarette.

2. Immediately shift your attention to your breath. You will notice that in such times of upset, your breathing is fast and shallow. Slow it down. Take slow, deep breaths. Puff up your stomach to inhale more air and contract it to expel all of it. Focus on the breath leaving your nostrils and, as it does, visualize the negative emotions also leaving in a dark stream.

    Visualize golden, strength-giving light streaming in with your inhalation. Keep doing this. Go into the "Witness" mode and watch your emotions writhing in a maelstrom. You will be pleasantly amazed by how fast your negative emotions will dissipate.

    You will find that music has a profound effect on your mood. Classical music—Mozart, Beethoven, Bach—is very calming. Try Gregorian chants, Islamic calls to prayer, Buddhist temple music, or similar sounds as well.

Exercise: Your Ideal Job

Craft a description of your ideal job.

Please take this exercise very seriously and devote a great deal of thought to it. Invest enough emotional energy in your writing that it literally becomes a statement of purpose to the Universe. It should be your intention to manifest what you are writing some-time in the not too distant future.

I am making the assertion that the ideal job, the one that you are seeking, DOES NOT EXIST. You have to, quite literally, create it and assemble it in bits and pieces. You will have a better chance of succeeding if you clearly know what you are trying to do.

Write in the present tense. "I work in a . . ." rather than "I will work in a . . ." See yourself, as vividly as you can, actually living the life you are writing about.

There are several levels to your task. There is the environment. Where is it? What type of building, office, furniture, setting, etc.? Do you travel? Where and how much? With whom do you interact? What is the nature of the interaction? Do you have transactions with many, changing individuals or do you develop long-term relations with a few?

Explicitly recognize contradictions. If you want to discuss Shakespearean sonnets with your coworkers, don't become a stevedore. It's not that English literature majors never become stevedores, it's simply that the probabilities are against it. You might see yourself as the kind of person who radically changes his/her environment. The kind of person who, when put in a boiler room, will have everyone interested in sonnets in short order. If this is the case, mention it explicitly.

What is the culture of the organization you work for? How is it expressed? Is this one that you are comfortable with? What kind of people are your coworkers? Your boss? His or her bosses? Do you have any type of genuine social relations with anyone from work?

What skills and talents do you possess and how do you use them in your job? What new skills and talents do you acquire? How?

What are the core values of your life and how do you express them in your job? Do you see conflicts? How do you resolve them?

Who benefits from you doing what you do? Consider both direct and indirect benefits. How deep does the cycle of connectedness extend? How deeply do you wish to follow it? Who do you wish to benefit and how?

Does what you are doing contribute in any way to the larger good of the world as you see it? Lessening of violence, reduction of environmental despoliation, greater equity, more self-sufficiency for all, etc.? To what do you want to make a contribution? Are you satisfied with what you are doing?

Do you have a family? How does your family fit into all this? What are the trade-offs and how do you handle them?

Last, but not least, in what way is what you do an expression of who you are? How does it fit into your notion of spiritual life?

It is my sincere hope that this assignment is something you will continue working on for the rest of your life.

HELPFUL HINTS

Many report that when they sit down to write about their ideal job, their mind is blank. They have no idea what stirs their passion, no idea of what they would really like to do. So they don't do the exercise.

Big mistake. This is an exercise that should be repeated every four to six months. It may take many such iterations before any kind of clarity begins to appear. If you find yourself stuck, just put pen to paper and start writing furiously. Write fast, without thinking, in a stream of consciousness. Such fast writing dissolves the blocks erected by your thinking, rational mind and brings to the surface the latent thoughts and passions that you harbor.

Examine yourself as you are writing. When you start coming alive with possibility, when the pen moves almost by its own volition and you become breathless at the thought of achieving the life you are writing about, when you could go on forever because what you are doing seems so "right" to you, that is when you have achieved the breakthrough you are looking for. And that is when the life you are imagining will start manifesting in bits and pieces. It is your task to assemble all the pieces, and this could take the rest of your life.

Good luck! That is what this journey is all about!

CHAPTER EIGHT

YOU ALWAYS ACT IN YOUR SELF-INTEREST—EVERYONE DOES!

—➤◦◄—

In this chapter, you will discover the secret of how work can become a joy and how to make success dog your footsteps. To get to this happy state, you will have to put down two enormous boulders that you have unthinkingly shouldered. One is guilt and the other is blame. These are connected with a strong cord, like the stones of a bola, the throwing weapon of the Argentine gaucho. You can put them both down at the same time.

AN EXCERPT FROM A GLOBAL BUSINESS INTERVIEW WITH ARTHIK DHARMATMA, CEO OF GENERAL TECHNOLOGIES

> **G.B.:** Congratulations on your retirement! In twenty-two
> years at the helm of GT, you have increased market
> capitalization by more than any other CEO in history
> while simultaneously maintaining a reputation as the

most ethical executive around. Our readers are really
interested in what you have to say.

A.D.: *Thank you. I am glad to share what I know, but I am
not sure I have anything to say that your readers will find
valuable.*

G.B.: Let's talk about ethics. Have you faced any dilemmas?
Have you done anything you regret?

A.D.: *Sure I've faced dilemmas. Choosing between what is
right and what is wrong is easy. The tough ones are when
you are confronted with choices that are both right.
Sometimes that can really hurt.*

G.B.: Give us an example.

A.D.: *We hit an economic downturn during my first stint
as a manager. My boss and I made a list of people who
would have to be let go, but we were keeping it quiet
because a customer was considering a big order and that
could have changed things. One of my direct reports, a
high school classmate, had just gotten married and was
about to buy a house.*

*He knew there would be layoffs and asked me if he
would be okay. He wanted to know before he signed for a
mortgage. I knew he was on the list to be let go, but
couldn't tell him. I did say that, in my opinion, it would
not be a good idea to go in for a big financial commitment
when there was so much uncertainty. However, since I did
not tell him that he was out, he signed for the mortgage.*

The order did not come through and he was laid off the next week.

He never spoke to me again.

G.B.: *That must still cause you pain! How about another example?*

A.D.: *Okay. This one happened later in my career. I was heading a money-losing division and my boss was under a lot of pressure. Other units were doing even worse and he just didn't want to have a discussion on options. He gave me a choice: Either I made a profit or he would shut down the operation, throwing everyone out of work, including myself.*

The retiree pension fund was sitting on unrealized gains and the accountants made some very aggressive assumptions about future rates of return. I signed off on it and we took several million dollars back, and that just got us into the black. The division was saved. But I knew we would never make the assumed returns and we did not. We had to terminate the plan two years later and a lot of retirees were left hanging—people who had spent years with the company and thought they were provided for.

G.B.: *Do you feel guilty?*

A.D.: *I did for years. Sometimes I could hardly sleep because of a hard knot in my stomach. It took a long time before I could put the guilt down.*

Right at this moment, you are carrying a load of guilt on your shoulders, just as A.D. did. In despondent moments you think about the things you have done wrong and then pick up your trusty knobbed walking stick and beat yourself bloody.

The number of things for which you berate yourself is legion. You are not a good son or daughter; you've caused great pain to your parents; you haven't been a perfect parent/spouse/friend/neighbor; you've flubbed important interviews/projects/presentations; you've been drinking/smoking/eating/indulging too much; you haven't made the most of opportunities; you've tried too hard; you haven't tried hard enough; and you are just being/doing/getting something or other. You are always making resolutions, always trying to "fix" your so obvious and glaring shortcomings, and always failing.

Think of how much of your mental chatter is devoted to running yourself down for what you did that you shouldn't have done, or what you didn't do that you should have.

There is another load you carry. For many this is equally heavy. This one is blame. If you are in a sorry situation, you blame all and sundry. Your parents loom large in this blame game. They are "responsible" for everything from your poor self-esteem to your lack of occupational skills. Spouses, former spouses, and significant others are also likely culprits. They have, in their various ways, "ruined" your life. In-laws have a starring role in the movie of what makes you miserable. And let's not forget children, relatives, coworkers, bosses, politicians, and innumerable others. Their thoughtless and/or malicious acts have caused and are causing you untold grief. It's all their fault!

Guilt and blame are terrible burdens to carry. Not only that, but as long as you are carrying them, your hands are not free to pick up the better things in life. The good news is that you *can* become free of guilt and blame. In fact, the truth you are about to learn will cause them to lighten, then dissipate like early morning fog in a tropical summer.

LAWS OF NATURE

There are some things that we recognize are Laws of Nature. They are fixed and immutable. They just *are*. You don't question them. You don't argue with them. You don't waste your energy trying to change or fix them. You just accept them and adjust your life to accommodate them.

The Law of Gravity is one such Law. If you drop an object, you know it will fall to the ground. Let's say you are interested in photography and have just bought a $4,000 digital camera. It has bells and whistles and you are really proud of it. You are far up on a cliff and see a gorgeous bird with orange and red plumage on a ledge below you. You lean over and fiddle with the controls to get a close-up. Your fingers slip and the camera plummets to the earth far below.

What happens now? You certainly feel bad. You might kick yourself for being foolish enough to lean over the edge without putting the camera strap around your neck or using some such safety mechanism. You might reflect on how this is merely the latest in the very long list of dumb things you have done, and how you are doomed to failure and thus starvation because you seem to have an inability to learn. From here you then slide rapidly into a downward spiral. You might blame friends or traveling companions for suggesting you buy such an expensive camera, or for setting up the climb, or for somehow being responsible for your loss.

Or you might shrug your shoulders and write it off as an expensive lesson. You may decide to go on a diet of crackers and water till you have saved enough to replace the camera, or you may decide that you simply do not want to get another such expensive device. You may feel sad for two weeks, or ten minutes, or not at all.

One thing will *not* happen. You will *not* rail against the Law of Gravity. You will not pound your fists on the wall and scream at the Law, "Why did you have to do this? Didn't you realize that this was a hugely expensive camera and very important to me? Why couldn't you just relax your effect this one time so the camera remained floating for a few seconds when it slipped from my hand? Why did you do this to me, you horrible creature you?"

It will not happen because you accept the Law of Gravity. You *always* have. It is there. It has always been there. So you work and shape your life around it.

There is another law that is almost as immutable as the Law of Gravity. However, you have never understood this. You have not recognized it as a law that shapes your behavior and everybody else's. Because of this ignorance, you have picked up and carried the huge loads of guilt mentioned earlier. Because of this ignorance, you blame others for your misfortunes and resent them bitterly.

If you understand this law, you will accept it. Once you do, there will be no more guilt in your life and you will cease blaming others. And there's a bonus: You will cease blaming yourself! A large part of guilt consists of turning that blame inward and this, too, will go away. So will the other parts. You will simply accept yourself and stop beating up on yourself so mercilessly.

The Law of Self-interest

Ready? Here goes: *Everybody, at all times, ALWAYS acts in his or her perceived self-interest.*

It bears repeating, with emphasis: ***Everybody, at all times, ALWAYS acts in his or her perceived self-interest.***

Right now you are puzzled. You don't understand this "Law,"

you disagree with what you *think* you understand, and you sure don't see how what I've just told you will rid you of the burdens you are carrying.

Let's start with your disagreement. Your mental chatter is probably telling you, "There's some truth to what he says. But only some. I *am* doing stuff for myself some of the time, probably much of the time, but I am *not* selfish. In fact, I am pretty altruistic. More so than most, actually." In this vein, you proceed to mentally list all the things you do for others. The number of times you drive your son and his friends to soccer games, the dinner you cooked for your spouse's parents, the volunteer work you do at the local soup kitchen, the helping hand you always lend to coworkers in a spot, and so on.

In fact, by the time you finish your list, you probably feel like a paragon of virtue.

First a story. This one features the author G. K. Chesterton and the playwright George Bernard Shaw. Don't bother checking it for historical accuracy.

Chesterton and Shaw were deep in conversation as they took a ride in their horse-drawn carriage. The argument was getting heated. Chesterton maintained that a country could only prosper when its politicians were altruistic and acted to bring about broader good. Shaw averred that there was no such thing as altruism, that people were inherently selfish and acted in their own interest.

They passed a pig stuck in a fence and it was squealing piteously. Nails had given way and a heavy wooden bar had slipped, pinning the pig's head to the bar below. It was raining hard and the ditch through which the fence ran was filling with water. It would not be too long before the pig drowned.

Shaw, still arguing, asked the coachman to stop. He clambered out *and made his way to the animal, lifted the fallen bar, and set the pig free. It dashed off. Shaw fell as he turned back. His greatcoat was muddy and his top hat was dented and water gushed from his once fashionable shoes.*

Chesterton ostentatiously held his nose and spread newspapers for Shaw to sit on so he would not ruin the expensive upholstery. Then he closed in for the kill.

"You just proved my point!" he exclaimed triumphantly. "There was an altruistic act if ever I saw one. You ruined a perfectly good set of clothes to set that animal free."

"On the contrary," said Shaw imperturbably as he tried ineffectually to dry himself with a sodden handkerchief. "It was a purely selfish act. If I had not set the pig free, I would not have been able to sleep tonight wondering if it had managed to escape."

Shaw was on to something. Do you feel good because you are doing wonderful things for your significant other? It's because what you do reinforces the image you have of how a husband or wife should behave. It is amazing how fast the good feelings—and actions—dissipate if the other party does not reciprocate as you expect. That's why divorce rates are so high!

Let's look at some common examples of our hidden moments of self-interest. Do you get up early in the morning to make lunch for your kids as they head out to school? It's because you have a notion of what parents should do and you are trying to live up to it. Are you a sucker for hard-luck stories and always reaching for your wallet as you read about horrible disasters in distant parts of the world? It's because you think of yourself as a compassionate person and have to act in conformity with it.

None of this is a secret. Much "philanthropy" is an elaborate dance in which supplicant institutions find new ways to cater to the egos of wealthy individuals by demonstrating that they "can make a difference." The organizations put the donors' names on programs and on buildings. They set up bronze statues and publicly acknowledge their benefactors' contributions in various ways. It's a simple swap—money for elaborate and sophisticated ego gratification.

Do you make anonymous contributions to your favorite charities? It's because you have a firm idea of what the world should be like, and it isn't that way. The charities you support are doing their part to bring about your view, and aiding them relieves the tension in you. Do you give generously whenever there is an earthquake, flood, fire, storm, or other natural disaster? Do you donate to alleviate the suffering of innocents caught up in the genocidal wars that still rage on our planet? As unlikely as it seems, all your giving is self-centered. You give because it makes you feel good about your actions and proud of your good nature. That is why you are willing to contribute and to sacrifice.

You are acting in your perceived self-interest. You always do. Everyone always does. It's a Law of Nature.

Wait a minute here, you think. Are you saying that *everything* I do is in some sense "selfish" because the reason I do it is to get some level of emotional satisfaction and relief? That is exactly what I am saying. And the knowledge of this truth is both wonderful and liberating, even if it doesn't seem like it at first.

But it is liberating *only* if you understand and accept it at a very deep level.

Exercise: Drop Your Camera

Take a moment and think of three things you regret having done. The "should haves" and the "why didn't Is?" Think of how, when you did them, you were acting in your perceived best interest.

Today, with greater maturity, you may clearly see that what you then thought was in your best interest really wasn't. But you did not know it then. Clearly see that you were like a child who grabs a red-hot poker. You don't blame the child. He just did not know any better. He was fascinated by the glow and reached out for it with no knowledge that it would hurt. Clearly understand that you were exactly like that child. Blaming yourself is like blaming the Law of Gravity for letting your camera fall. You just don't do it. You just can't do it.

Do this exercise for a few days and you will see that your burden of guilt lightens and then slips away.

Now for part two of the exercise. Make a list of all those people whom you blame. Those people who did you wrong. Those who did so many things to make your life miserable in so many ways. They, too, were acting in their perceived self-interest. Each and every one of them. Maybe you thought they were wrong. Maybe some of them now think they were wrong. Maybe they think they were right or maybe they don't think about it at all. It doesn't matter. At the time they did what they did, at the time they caused you the pain, anguish, or aggravation, they were acting just as you acted—in their perceived self-interest. It's a Law of Nature. Blaming them is like blaming the Law of Gravity for letting your camera fall. You just don't do it. You just can't do it.

And so you set down the boulder of blame.

HELPFUL HINT

The story below clarifies the point further. You may find it helpful.

He was close to the end of a long and virtuous life but just could not forget things he had done in his youth that had hurt himself and others.

So deep and poignant was his sorrow that the Master decided to inter-vene and touched him on the forehead.

Instantly he was transported to a museum with wondrous paintings and works of art. But wait! There was something wrong. Many of the pictures were defaced. Some had ink spilled on them, some had knife slashes, and some were torn. Some statues were similarly broken, or tarred, or burnt.

He felt himself going back through time and saw a young child with an innocent mien romping through the museum. The child laughed with joy as he saw the pictures surrounding him. He saw a knife and plunged it through the frame of a nearby painting. He knocked a statue off a pedestal and clapped his hands with joy as it fell and shattered. He saw matches and looked around for what would serve as fuel for a fire.

He looked more closely at the face of the child and, in horror, recog-nized himself. And, in a flash, he understood why the Master had sent him there.

"That's right, my son," confirmed the Master. "You were the one who did the damage. You did it because you did not know what you were do-ing. It's no use blaming the child. He did what gave him momentary pleasure at the time.

"Go back and make what restitution you can. If you spilled ink on a painting, you can erase it with care. If you burnt a statue, there is noth-ing that can be done. Learn from your mistakes and move on. There is never any turning back on the path we call Life."

When you castigate the young child who was you, you go on the guilt trip. When you castigate the young child who was some-one else, you go on the blame trip. Both are painful diversions on life's journey, and you will avoid them if you realize that everybody, at all times, always acts in his or her perceived self-interest. Even you. Especially you.

This is a very tough concept to grasp and internalize because it is so contrary to the beliefs you probably have. That's okay. Practice the exercises above frequently. Examine yourself, your motives, and your mental chatter as you do things that you think are altruistic. Gradually you will see the truth of this for yourself.

Remember that, ultimately, you are mastering these principles for yourself. You are *not* doing it for someone else. When you carry anger, or guilt, or blame inside you, the only person you are damaging is yourself. The Law described above is a neat method of putting down this heavy burden.

THE UNIVERSE IS A FORCE MULTIPLIER

From the Law of Increase, you learned that whatever you are truly grateful for and appreciate will increase in your life. There is a dark flip side to this. The negative emotions you broadcast—anger, hate, distrust, and the like—are also picked up and reflected back to you with greater force.

The Universe is like a very sensitive and powerful amplifier. It picks up what you emit, greatly increases its power, and beams it back to you. At some level you understand this and it is certainly a part of the common wisdom embodied in sayings like "What goes around, comes around," "You reap what you sow," and "It's payback time."

In military parlance, a force multiplier is something that greatly enhances the effectiveness of any weapon or military tactic. Bombs are effective. Precision-guided bombs are more effective. Precision-guided bombs that are led to their exact destination by a spotter on the ground with a laser-targeting device are orders of magnitude more effective. The ground spotter is a force multiplier, and because of him—or her—fewer bombs need to be used, they can be less powerful, and there is less loss of innocent life.

The Universe is a giant force multiplier, and you can learn to harness its immense power. You have been using it unconsciously and, thus, frequently unwisely. I now invite you to use it both consciously and wisely. The way you use it is by understanding how it operates and by controlling the broadcast you make that it picks up and amplifies back to you.

It will take very little time for you to notice the tremendous positive change in your life. In fact, you have already had some experience of this. The appreciation and gratitude exercise you have already done is an example of this principle at work.

I HATE MY JOB

The best way to explain this is with an example. Here is a very common situation I run into: "I hate my job! I get up in the morning and it is a physical dread. My boss is a tyrant, always picking on me and making sarcastic comments. He is incompetent, steals credit, and blames everyone else for his mistakes. The work is boring and there is too much of it since the last round of layoffs. My coworkers are ignorant, backbiting, and selfish. The people who report to me directly are dumb and disloyal. The customers are a pain in the backside—always demanding, and downright unreasonable. I'd gladly gum up the place if I thought I could get away with it."

Can you relate to any part of this?

First, recognize the stress you are experiencing and remember that *all* of it comes from the fact that you are living in a me-

larly feel grateful for each job-related piece. For the tough project from which you learned a lot. For the incessant travel that is making family life difficult but lets you work out regularly at hotel gyms. For the officer's post at the trade association that takes a lot of time but also gets you known in the industry.

Feel the appreciation emanate out and envelop you.

Recognize that the frustration you feel is because you have spent and are spending all your energy focusing on what you don't have. On the things that trouble you in your workplace. On stuff that you would change by force if you could. This is a hallmark of a me-centered universe.

Focus instead on what is right with your place of work. You can't do it all the time, but do it as much as you can. Really do it. Put your heart in it.

Do you think of yourself as a meaningless cog in a giant gear wheel? Don't. The enterprise in which you work is conveying real benefits to someone, somewhere. There are households that are functioning because of the salaries it provides, there are communities that offer services because of the taxes it pays, there are customers whose lives are better because of the products it puts out.

Think of the vast web of connections—with customers, vendors, communities, the public, the government—that you are a small part of. Does your company make the cables that go into the braking systems of airplanes? Then you have a small role in helping millions of passengers travel safely for vacations and for business. Be grateful for this.

A magnificent cathedral was going up. Already it dwarfed structures in the entire country and it had not reached half its intended elevation or a quarter of the land it would cover. The incomparable frescos, the marvelous stained-glass windows, the ornate carvings—these were all still notions in the minds of the architect and the cabal of master craftsmen he had assembled.

As the architect walked along the dusty road to inspect his creation unfolding, he passed three men toiling in the hot noonday sun. Each was a young man in the prime of life. Each was performing the same task. A painful, laborious task. Each would take a piece of rock, put it on a large flat stone, and hit it with a sledgehammer till it broke. To each he posed the same question, "What are you doing, my good man, and why are you doing it?"

The first man answered: "Can't you see what I am doing? I am breaking rocks and I do it because I get ha'pennoth a day."

The second man answered: "I am making the small stones that will go into the wall of yonder building. I do it so I can feed my family."

The third man answered: "I am helping construct this wondrous cathedral you see before you. When it is finished, people will come here from many countries to gaze upon its marvels. I do it so I can learn how, for, truth to tell, I can earn a better wage with less effort as an apprentice."

On an impulse the architect summoned his assistant and asked him to keep track of each of the men over the years.

Four decades later, the first man had died. He had remained a day laborer working at even more menial tasks when his strength eroded. The second man had retired and was living in modest comfort. He had, in time, become a craftsman and achieved a reputation as a dependable, if unimaginative, worker.

The third man? The architect had no need to ask about him. His fame was still spreading, and the wondrous edifices he had conceived of dotted the land.

DON'T break rocks that go into a wall. Be part of a team that builds a cathedral. Even the water bearer in a caravan contributes to its success. It's all in your head.

When you have done all this, it is time for the next step. Identify one area in your work where you would like to improve your skills and become more efficient. This should involve some learning on your part. Pick something where your success will result in increasing the part of your work you most enjoy.

Are you a financial planner who really hates cold calling but who loves writing? Learn about direct mail and how to create compelling headlines and copy so you can spend more time with clients and less time trying to get appointments. Are you a boss who dislikes telling subordinates that they are not pulling their weight but likes supporting your staff? Take a course on Socratic questioning and providing effective feedback. Do you wish you could stick up for yourself more when aggressive coworkers invade your turf and "assign" you tasks you would rather not do? Go to a seminar on assertiveness training or nonviolent communication. Do you like dealing with clients who really respect your knowledge and the care with which you provide services to them? Analyze your favorite clients, develop a profile, and come up with a strategy for getting more of them.

For one month focus exclusively on acquiring the skill you have identified and applying it appropriately. The learning is important. You have to learn something that gets you out of familiar territory and increases your knowledge base and your skill set. You will select the learning and the measure used for evaluation.

If you are the financial planner learning about direct mail, for example, you may set a goal of learning what makes a headline effective and how to compose a powerful one as your learning objective. Coming up with at least ten headlines for the service you provide might be your performance goal.

Evaluate your progress at the end of the month. If you have not met your goals, it may be because you need more time, or more resources, or because your target was inappropriate. Set another target skill and performance goal for the second month. It's okay to extend the previous month's targets if you need more time and you have made progress. It's not okay to do this simply because you did not make an honest effort and therefore did not accomplish anything.

You will often find that you are stuck and need to reach out to others who have the knowledge and skills you lack. By all means, extend yourself. The next exercise gives you powerful methods to elicit such help. Be persistent.

Keep doing this for a year. At the end of this time, you will have learned at least a half dozen new skills and improved your performance on many functions. But more important, you will have rejuvenated your job. Not only that, I will wager you dinner that you will also find that your job performance has improved greatly and that you are actually enjoying it much of the time.

Your increased satisfaction comes about for two reasons. You have acted in your self-interest but you have also expanded your understanding of self-interest. What you are really doing is using the Law of Increase and the knowledge of the Universe as a force multiplier to your advantage. When you stop explicitly focusing on yourself, on what you want and what you don't have, and start focusing on how you can be of service to a larger community, then you set loose some very powerful forces. Your broadcast goes out, gets amplified, and comes right back to you. In fact, this is the most efficient method of truly getting the happiness that you crave.

When you first try this, you may feel that you are playacting. You don't really feel sincere about being of service to others. That's okay. You cannot overcome the "me-first" conditioning of decades immediately. Keep playacting. Sooner or later, like the amateur actor mentioned earlier, you will begin to sink into your role.

And that is when your life begins to take off!

Try it.

HELPFUL HINTS

1. Remember that focus is the key. Your job makes you miserable if you focus on the myriad things that are "wrong" with it. You can start making it totally rejuvenating when you begin by focusing on what is "right" with it. Ignore all the stuff—even if it is the vast majority—that you feel is "wrong."

2. You will have many people tell you that when you ignore the "horrible" things at work, you are actually helping them continue and perpetuating the status quo. They might even accuse you of actually "helping" the organization get away with all sorts of bad behavior. Ignore all of this. You are doing this for you, not for the company you work for. You always work in your perceived best self-interest. Make this work for you!

Now that you understand that everyone works in their own self-interest, you can have a very different perspective on professional relationships. You don't worry about what others will think when you interact with them—they are doing exactly whatever it is they need to do on their own behalf!

Take this new understanding into your web of work relationships. Networks are important. Formal networks exist in organization charts and similar hierarchies. Informal networks exist as affinity groups, circles of friends and relatives, and many other similar associations. The latter are far more important and are what you draw on to "get the job done." You rely on informal networks to get the skinny on the company you are considering joining, the employee you want to hire, or the best restaurant for an important luncheon meeting.

There are books, courses, and seminars on networking. I have long had a problem with the notion that you should cultivate a person based on the help that you could potentially receive sometime in the future. This is the kind of thinking that encourages you to identify a politician as a "comer" and get to know him or her before their actual "coming." The same dynamic occurs with rising business executives or star performers in any field. Too often, you make a judgment on the running potential of the steed and then decide whether or not to invest time in cultivating it. Bah!

Treating people this way is artificial, superficial, and cheapening. There is no depth or true warmth in such relationships, and you cannot rely on them. In my opinion, there is only one good reason for cultivating a relationship with someone. Something about that person, preferably a positive value he or she expresses in some manner, touches a deeply responsive chord in you. You will, of course, deal with all people appropriately in professional situations whether or not you relate to them in this way. But you will cultivate only those who, in some important respect, are kindred spirits.

People always drop clues about who they really are, and it is easy to pick up on them if you are sensitive and attuned. Do you want to find out if a CEO really believes in teamwork? Read his or her speeches and discover whether the tenor is "*We* did it" or "*I* did it." Read proxy statements to ascertain if bonuses are carefully hoarded or are widely distributed. Tap insiders to determine if "executive perks" are jealously and secretly guarded. There are many ways to find out. All that is needed is the ability to pick up on subtle clues. Fortunately, this is a skill that is easily learned. You simply have to become consciously aware of what you are looking for.

Once you think you have detected such a clue, you will drop some of your own and see if they are, in turn, picked up. You will investigate in other ways, but discreetly. As you gain practice, you will be amazed by how easy and accurate it is.

Exercise: A New Take on Networking!

Pick five people you would like to cultivate. They can be anywhere. They can be people you already know or those about whom you are aware. They could be friends or relatives, professional colleagues and business acquaintances, sports partners and fellow hobbyists.

Figure out what it is about that person that resonates within you. What you admire about them. Which of their values, accomplishments, behaviors, impressed you. You are going to write a letter to or take an action that involves each one of these people. Let each person know what it is that touches you and why. Be concise; don't be fulsome. But you have to write from your heart. If you don't have utter sincerity, it will not work.

State a specific way in which you can help or would like to be useful to that person. Spend time coming up with creative ways to do this. They should not be trivial or banal. Make sure you are, fully and honestly, prepared to follow through on the help you offered. If you are not so prepared, don't do it.

There are many ways in which you can do this.

1. You notice a journalist who has written a number of pieces exposing malfeasance in business. She has, fearlessly and possibly at personal risk, attacked powerful icons. You feel that what she is doing badly needs to be done. You write her a sincere note of congratulations. You then tell her about dishonest/illegal/immoral practices in an industry that you have become aware of through a relative. Offer to set her up with sources if she wants to investigate further.

2. You learn through the company newsletter that an executive in another department is trying to organize a group to "adopt" an inner-city basketball team. Offer to join and also to recruit others.

3. An executive speaks up at a trade association meeting about deceptive marketing practices in your industry. Talk to him about action steps that can be taken to eliminate them and what you can contribute. Let him know that he is not alone.

Use any form of communication that you feel comfortable with. E-mail is fast and convenient. You can also write, phone, fax, and send instant messages. It's okay to be creative. If you want to hire a plane to skywrite a message above the person's front lawn, go right ahead. But you will probably find this expensive and unsuitable for long messages.

What's Inside You?

Rossagollas are traditional Indian sweets. They are round and white, about the size of a Ping-Pong ball, and are much beloved by young and old. If you squeeze a *rossagolla*, what comes out is sweet, sweet syrup. It does not matter how you squeeze it. You can do it between thumb and forefinger. You can drop it on a hard floor and step on it. You can run over it with a truck. You can put a suitcase down on it. In every case it yields the sugary solution that has rested in it.

Why does the sweet stuff come out from a *rossagolla* even when it is treated so horribly? Because that's what is in it!

Life has different ways of putting the squeeze on you—work-related pressure, family discord, health issues, political discomfiture. What comes out of you when you are squeezed? In all likelihood it isn't going to be sweet syrup. More likely it's going to be a sticky sap of guilt, depression, envy, worry, unhappiness, shame, sorrow, nervousness, jealousy, hate, fear, embarrassment, or frustration. Why? Because that is what is inside you. These emotions do not come from outside. They are within you all the time. The nasty stuff that emerges when you are squeezed is the beast you have been feeding.

Steve loathed his boss, Bob, with a passion. Everything about Bob annoyed him. His habit of dressing sharply—"What a fop!"—his cheerful greeting of the administrative assistants—"Buttering them up so he can get them to work after office hours!"—and the way he carefully considered all aspects of a situation before taking action—"Can't make a fast decision if his life depends on it. However did he become a division manager?"

Steve also disliked the company he worked for. He thought it was not prestigious enough for a person of his talents and deeply resented that he was unable to get a job with a better-known company. He railed at everything, from the wallpaper scheme to the quality of office supplies. He tried to keep it under control, but the dislike would frequently show itself in snide, sarcastic comments.

After work hours one evening, Steve was returning from the coffee machine when he saw that though Bob's door was closed, he could hear voices coming from inside Bob's office. Somehow the speaker button on the secretary's desk had been activated and he could hear the conversation. There was no one else around, so he pretended to be searching for a file in a cabinet nearby.

". . . has to be let go now," an unseen voice said. He did not recognize it.

"What's the best way to handle it?" asked Bob.

"Best done on a Friday evening," counseled the voice. "Make sure the report is on your table before . . ." Steve heard movement in the passageway and slipped noiselessly into his office, seething with rage. Bob was going to fire him!

When Bob called him to his office that Friday evening and asked him to bring the product-launch file, Steve was bitter and prepared. Throwing the unfinished report on Bob's table, he burst out, "No, you don't get to fire me. I quit. You hear me? I quit. I wouldn't want to work in a dump like this anyway." He proceeded to tell Bob exactly what he thought of him. He was intemperate and abusive.

Bob listened without any reaction. Steve paused for breath as his tirade ran down. Then Bob spoke, and his voice was gentle. "I had to let Ralph go today. I called you in to ask you to fill his spot. That would have been a big promotion, but I thought you could handle it and even thought it would make you feel better about the company. I needed to be briefed on the product-launch project so I could ask Abigail to take over.

"You know, Steve, you are very bright and a darn good worker," Bob continued, "but your attitude brings you down every time. I tried to cut you all the slack I could. None of what you said today bothered me except one thing. If you refer to the place you work in as a 'dump,' you

really don't belong here. It's your job to make it better, not to run it down. Thanks for quitting. Don't make the same mistake wherever you go next."

Steve never recognized that his condemnatory mental chatter was actually nourishing the strongly negative impulses inside him. They burst out eventually and he did not like the consequences. It is more than likely that you, too, are unconsciously indulging in the same type of behavior to some extent, thus feeding the beasts you actually want to starve.

But it doesn't have to be this way. You can transform the gunk that is inside you and to which you are adding on a regular basis. Even decreasing the amount that you are adding daily will result in a quantum improvement in your life! You've already experienced the truth about this by performing the exercises in previous chapters—especially the appreciation and gratitude exercise.

All transformation begins and ends with mental models. Because these models dictate how you act under different circumstances and how you interpret the events that happen in your life, when you change the model, you change your life. As we have seen, we all have models that are healthy and wonderful and those that are painful and poisonous. It is time to get rid of the latter.

The way to real personal mastery is to sweep away those models that block the goodness inside you so that all the sweet syrup flows when life gets tough.

After many years at the helm, the Abbot of the monastery knew that it was time for him to move on to the final phase of his life. He appointed his successor and, in the early morn, prepared to leave. His sim-

ple bundle contained only a change of clothes and a few cooking vessels. He had no need for more.

His successor was waiting with bare feet at the gate of the monastery. He pressed a package into the Abbot's hand and whispered, "This is our gift to you. There is no one who can make better use of it and no place where it has more usefulness than with you. Take it and bless us. There is only one condition—you may not open the package until you are seven days away from here." He left after prostrating.

On the eighth day, the Abbot opened the package and was stunned. It was a magnificent book, richly hand illustrated and full of the Blessed One's teachings. Many, many hours had he spent with it in bygone days. It was the greatest treasure of the monastery he had left. He instantly knew why he had been enjoined from opening the package until seven days' journey had passed. He would never have consented to receive it if he had known.

He settled down in a distant village and lived a quiet life of contemplation while he waited for his days to end. He studied the book daily, even though the contents were engraved in his mind, and it brought him much solace. He arranged with a trustworthy local youth to have it taken back to the monastery when his time was done.

One day a shifty-eyed traveler knocked at his door and received shelter and a share of his meager meal, as many had before him. When the Abbot rose before dawn, his visitor had gone and so had the book of teachings.

The thief traveled for three days and came to a town before he felt safe enough to sell his loot. The town scribe was the most learned man in the town and was also a merchant. The thief produced the book and asked for ten pieces of gold. He proclaimed that it was an ancient volume that had been in his family for generations and had been written by a venerable sage. The scribe examined it with awe. "If it is truly writ-

ten by the sage, it is worth every bit of ten gold pieces," he affirmed. He told the thief to come back in a week while he verified its authenticity.

When the thief returned, the scribe poured out a hundred pieces of gold in front of him. "No one here has the ability to authenticate such a treasure," he explained. "The former Abbot of a famous monastery resides in a village three days away and I sent my assistant to him with the book to inquire about its value. He readily confirmed its origins and said that were I to give less than a hundred pieces of gold for it, I would be guilty of thievery."

The thief changed his mind and reclaimed the book. He rushed back to the village he had left so hurriedly and the Abbot whose treasure he had spirited away. Throwing himself at the Abbot's feet, he begged for forgiveness. "Give me that which you have," he pleaded. "Give me that which enabled you to so readily give up a treasure of such value."

And so he became the Abbot's student and lived humbly close by and imbibed the teachings, and these took root in him. And one day the Abbot blessed him and departed his body. The erstwhile thief performed the last rites with tears in his eyes and then personally traveled to the monastery he had never seen to deliver the book that had inadvertently started him on his own quest.

He joined the monastery and stayed for many decades and, one day, in turn, became its Abbot.

What caused the Abbot to react so generously to what most of us would consider a grievous wrong? The same thing that once led the Buddha to bless the man who had laced his food with poison. The same thing that led Jesus on the cross to plead for forgiveness for his tormentors. Benevolence toward all was inside them, and that is what came out when they were squeezed.

But you can't get rid of the bad stuff simply by determining to do so. You *can* get rid of it by changing the mental models under which you operate. Healthier models allow more good into our lives, and as we focus on this goodness and use the Law of Increase, the bad stuff in our lives withers away.

Here is a general-purpose, all-inclusive "This is the way the world works" comprehensive model.

THE BENEVOLENT-UNIVERSE MODEL

> The Universe is a conscious and benevolent entity. It ALWAYS acts in your best interests and ALWAYS brings into your life EXACTLY what you need at any instant. Think of a complicated trapeze act. The aerialist lets go of the bar and does a dizzying array of twists and somersaults, and just as she finishes, the next bar is available for her to grasp. That's how the Universe acts. The bar you need is ALWAYS available just when you need it. The choreographing is both split-second and brilliant. The lesson you need to learn is exactly what you get at exactly the minute you need it. The resources you need are made available at the precise time that is appropriate. The people who come into your life are the very ones you need at the stage you are in. It is perfect. It has always been perfect, but you just never saw this. It will always be perfect in the future. All you have to do is relax and go with the flow.

Before you say, "Balderdash," or something quite a bit stronger, first take a deep breath. I realize that there is much here that is totally contradictory to how you "know" the world operates.

That is what your mental chatter is telling you. Try to let it go and bear with me for a while. You will not regret it.

Let's look at the principal objections to what I just said. First there is the notion of a "conscious" Universe and, further, a conscious Universe that is also "benevolent." This is probably quite far from how you view things. At best you probably think of the Universe as unaware of your existence and/or indifferent to it. At worst, you see it as fiendishly malevolent and single-mindedly working to thwart you in every possible way.

Then there is the notion that in the mammoth and immensely complicated world we live in, even tiny events are choreographed with you in mind. This is mind-boggling, even ludicrous. Also, this takes you into the "fate" versus "free will" domain. If the Universe is busy doing as indicated, then who are you, and what is your role, and what is your independence in that role?

There are many things that happen to you every day that you see as mildly good or mildly bad or just neutral: an unexpected bonus at the end of the year; the paper cut you get while making copies at the office; the quarter you spot on the street and pick up; the soup that contains more than a dollop of your favorite vegetable; the colleague who expresses sincere admiration for your work as she retires; the satisfaction you get from taking up Yoga and finally being able to touch your toes without bending your knees; the sinking feeling you get each morning when you step on the bathroom scales. We judge them all.

You are more likely to easily accept that the really good things that happen to you are gifts from a benevolent Universe (even if the gift is simply the ability to do the hard work required to get the good things)—the promotions at work, the prestigious awards, harmonious family relationships, and so on. But what about the really bad stuff that happens to you? The serious illness, the unexpected layoff, the untimely death of a loved one, the financial ruin, and so on? How can these be reconciled with the notion of a benevolent Universe? Worst of all is the horrible stuff that happens to you and involves another human being—possibly a young and innocent one. A young daughter who breaks her neck during gymnastics practice and becomes a quadriplegic, a son who gets blown up in a terrorist incident, a spouse stricken by Alzheimer's or Parkinson's disease, and so on. And, of course, to round out the list, there is the large-scale human tragedy that afflicts so many parts of the globe. Tragedy that has both natural and human causes and that involves large numbers of people.

All of these are genuine objections and I will address them, but before I do, let's get philosophical for a moment. Let's assume that the model proposed is utter garbage and the Universe really does not care about you. Or, worse, the Universe wakes up from time to time and actively stymies you. If you subscribe to this model, think of what it implies for you—the feeling of powerlessness, of vast unknown forces arrayed against you, of loneliness, of frustration and lack of control, and so on. This is not a pleasant house to live in.

What if you believed in the proposed benevolent model? You would feel no loneliness, because you would always be provided for in ways you cannot fathom. All sorrow would become bearable because it, somehow, would be for your good and your growth. There would be no frustration, because you would never be thwarted. Instead, you would feel that the Universe was simply charting a different and more efficient way to get you to where you needed to be.

A few minutes of reflection will convince you that, regardless of whether or not the proposed model is "true," *your* life would be immeasurably improved if you could sincerely adopt it. True or not, you would enjoy the benefits of the tranquility and sense of purpose the model provides.

And what if it really were "true"? What if the Universe was truly looking after your interests and, further, what if the more you believed this and were grateful, the more the bounty it showered on you? Then the phrase "heaven on earth" would take on a deeply personal meaning for you.

You *can* reach that place, starting right now. In fact, you have already begun the journey. All of the exercises in this book have broken down your old mental models and enabled you to replace them with more functional ones. This benevolent-universe proposed model simply ties them all together.

BELIEFS *CANNOT* BE FORCED

You cannot force yourself to adopt the proposed model. You may recognize intellectually that it is a good idea, but you cannot therefore automatically accept it.

Further, this model will be most helpful to you when you are under severe stress and dealing with the downside of the vicissitudes that life has a habit of tossing at you. But that is precisely the time when you cannot begin working with the model. You have to learn to surf and be pretty good at standing on a board *before* you can tackle the twenty-foot wave that comes your way.

It's the same with the proposed model. You cannot simply accept all of it at once. You have to work diligently at it, and it may take quite a while. However, the benefits begin immediately, and they rapidly become so great that it would be singularly foolish for you to shy away from the effort involved.

So what should you do?

You actively consider other perspectives and change what you focus on. You already had some experience with this when you practiced the creating-miracles exercise and contemplated the "Good Thing, Bad Thing" fable.

Exercise: Building Up to the Benevolent Universe Model

As you start to supplant old beliefs with the idea of the Benevolent Universe, I urge you to begin with your own personal history. Can you remember instances in your life when something happened that you initially labeled as terrible but that later opened up wonderful vistas? One of my students recalled that he desperately wanted an investment-banking summer job but was sick and in the hospital when the firms came to campus to recruit. He didn't have any job when summer started and was quite depressed. A friend of his father's, a physician, was going to one of the remotest and most poverty-stricken parts of Africa and invited him to tag along. With nothing better to do, he did.

For the first time in his life, he faced grinding deprivation and did without the "necessities" of life, like electricity and running water and indoor toilets. He also directly touched the lives of many people and experienced sincere and primal gratitude. He returned to Africa the next summer and then did a stint in the Peace Corps after graduation. His concept of what constituted a fulfilling job changed and he traversed a very different path from the one he imagined he would. He became deeply grateful for the illness that had kept him out of the interview circuit that spring.

Your examples may not be quite as dramatic or clear cut, but there are many such instances in your life. Identify each one and *write it down.* The act of recording is extremely important. You will not succeed in this endeavor if you do not take constant notes. When you write something down, it becomes reinforced in your mind. The written record gives you a means of going back to the incidents and noting how many there are. Both are crucial. When you have such a list, it is ever so much easier to go back to each experience and relive it, and this re-creation anchors it inside you.

As you look over your life, particularly seek instances when a "hidden hand" saved you from disaster. Here is an example. Three friends—all immigrants—lived together in New Jersey and commuted together to their jobs in New York. One day, as they were scrambling to get on a crowded train, a woman pushed through and cut one of them off. He cursed the delay because he was behind on his project. It was September 11, 2001, and all of them worked on one of the higher floors of the World Trade Center. He never made it to his office and he never saw his friends again. There are, once again, many such instances in your life, though probably not ones as amazing. Write each one down.

Consciously look for more such events in your life from now on. *Do not* be in a hurry to label something that happens to you as "terrible." Remember the "Good Thing, Bad Thing" story. Think of ways in which whatever happened might actually be a wonderful thing for you. Be fully prepared to act when you identify some path that might be opening up to you. Numerous attendees of my seminars have reported that common misfortunes like being fired from a job, the end of a relationship, unexpected illnesses, and so on led them to unexpected, but eventually more fulfilling, paths. Expect this to be true for you.

Gently entertain the possibility that the Universe really *is* looking out for you. Maybe yes, maybe no. Who knows? But try to be open to the possibility and always look for evidence to support it. Discard evidence that does not. Maybe the Universe *was* really supporting you but you just didn't recognize it.

Do this sincerely and you will be amazed by how many instances you find worth recording in your diary. Fill the pages and keep reviewing them. Do this at least once a day. As the notebook starts filling up and you keep reviewing it, you *will* come to a turning point. For some it will be a sharply defined one. For others it will be so gradual that they will know it only in hindsight. But you *will* get to a moment of decision, a true inflection point, if you have been diligent in both the observation and the recording of the observation.

When you arrive at that turning point, you will become acutely aware of the sheer number of instances where it seemed as if the Universe was working with and for you and in your best interests. You will face a decision—you can bring back your old models, the ones that made you so miserable, or you can carry on and go forward into uncharted territory. If you do the latter, miracles lie in store. You will look at your life and see, perhaps for the first time, that the Universe has been working on your behalf. You will seriously doubt that all of what has happened to you could have occurred by accident, that all of your experiences were "coincidences." For the first time it becomes easier to think of a conscious Universe that is helping you than to think it is an improbable string of fantastic happenstances.

This is the time for you to redouble your efforts. Do not slack off at this point, because if you do, you will easily give up all the ground you have gained and then some. Become more active, a lot more active, in terms of trying to see the hidden gifts in all the "misfortunes" that come your way. It will become easier and easier as you gain practice.

Steel is heated white hot and hammered and plunged into cold water on its way to becoming a fine sword. Think of the traumas that come your way as the human equivalent. They came to test you and stretch you and toughen you for the things you have to do in your life as you follow your unique path. Pay particular attention to the stories of others who faced great suffering that only served to take them to sublime heights.

Make it a point to read about winners of the various events in the Special Olympics, about businesspeople who snap back from bankruptcy and financial ruin, about social entrepreneurs, like Ashoka Fellows, who face overwhelming odds and chip away at them daily with unflagging fortitude. Paying attention to such tales will direct your own mental chatter and will make it easier for you to understand how the Universe is also shaping you in the same manner as the potter molds the wet clay.

As you practice this exercise—which I sincerely hope you do for the rest of your days—your life will be completely and utterly transformed.

COPING WITH SENSELESS TRAGEDIES

It is only *after* you have become thoroughly grounded in this new model that you can come to terms with such deep tragedies as the suffering of others. How can you reconcile the notion of a conscious, benevolent Universe with the knowledge of the horrific things that are happening in the world outside you? It is even tougher when horrible things happen to close loved ones.

There is a simple strategy that you can employ. Remember that it will work only if you have done the initial spadework and become comfortable with the concept that the Universe is constantly intervening in *your* life. That it is constantly steering you around pitfalls, bringing you the help you need when you feel overwhelmed, leading you to bounty in different guises, and always looking after you in myriad ways. You have to feel this at a very deep level before you can use the strategy presented below.

Think of a raging forest fire. It is beautiful in its vengeance if you are an observer far away from the heat and the searing flames. It destroys everything across vast swaths of land and possibly takes animal and human life as well. However, we now know that forest fires have their own necessary role in ecology. They thin trees, clear brush, and make it possible for new growth to occur. Accept that the tragedies you find difficult to fathom are like that forest fire in some way. The suffering is a painful cleansing. Recognize that the fact that the suffering disturbs you is a clear sign that your role is to do what you can to alleviate it and to work with others to lessen it. You cannot duck this responsibility.

That is the key. It bears repeating. *You cannot duck responsibility.* As long as the suffering moves you, you have to take some measure to lessen it and you have to do this consciously. Remember that this gets you right back to the other-centered-world exercise. You cannot, in the immortal words of Bob Dylan, turn your head and pretend that you just don't see. And if you act in this manner, providing succor without the drive of your ego needs, you will see how all tragedies fit into a grander scheme. Even if you do not see this clearly, you will sense that there is a larger purpose that is being served and that there is healing in this knowledge.

It is wonderfully liberating to live in this world. This world where the Universe behaves as if it were specifically designed for you and acts to give you exactly what you need. A world where you can accept that what you want is not always what you need. That a child may want a tub of ice cream but that a wise parent provides fresh fruit and vegetables.

Are you kidding yourself that the Universe is like this? Yes you are! You absolutely are!

But then you are kidding yourself that the Universe is the way you think it is right now—indifferent to you, and capricious with its gifts, and sometimes downright malicious.

You cannot "prove" either model. You cannot force yourself to believe either model. But you *can* let that belief arise in you. Do you want to dwell in a peaceful abode, with a deep sense of fulfillment and purpose? Or do you want to wander the corridors of a House of Horrors where ghastly apparitions appear without notice? It's your choice. And only your choice. And it is far, far better to live in the bosom of a benevolent Universe.

The exercises in this book have led you unfailingly in the direction of greater joy and certitude. If you have done them sincerely and consciously, they will have placed you on a path where each summit with its glorious view is quickly supplanted by a higher peak with an even more splendid vista.

That's just the way personal mastery works. Don't take my word for it. You would be foolish to. Discover it for yourself in your own life. *That* is when it will become a concrete reality for you. The "reality" that you will live in for the rest of your life.

He was a powerful Emperor, known for his justice and benevolence. He was wise beyond measure and governed so well that the kingdom prospered mightily and was constantly expanding even without military conquest. Village after village at the geographic frontiers simply elected to become part of the kingdom and the Emperor was too kind-hearted to refuse. His credo was that riches existed to be shared.

By custom, all members of any village that became a new part of the empire were welcome to visit the Royal Palace, in the capital. Each member of the palace staff to whom a villager paid respects was obligated to give a gift. The higher the position of the member, the more valuable was the gift given. This was the tradition, and it was widely proclaimed and known by all. It probably contributed to the willingness of villagers to merge with the kingdom.

The head man of a dirt-poor village that had just joined the kingdom was exhorting the villagers to set out for the capital. "It is so far," they wailed, "how can we leave our homes for so long? What will we eat on the way, and where will we find shelter, and what will become of our huts?" And so half the village did not even begin the journey.

The path was not well marked and the journey was long and arduous; half of those who set out lost heart and turned back. The rest struggled on and supported each other with words of encouragement, and they finally reached the capital.

The guard at the palace gate was tall and imposing. He wore a white-and-red uniform with gold braids and shiny brass buttons. The villagers had never seen anyone so impressive. "Surely this is the Emperor," they said, and they made obeisance to him. He gave each villager who did a handful of copper coins and they were satisfied. Many turned back to their village clutching the coins.

A few went up to the gate and the guard opened it for them. Inside was an usher, and he wore a similar uniform, but his clothes were made of silk and were more elegant. The villagers knew that they had been mistaken, that he was the Emperor, and they bowed. He gave them each a silver coin and many accepted it gratefully and took their leave.

The head man gathered his courage and asked if he was truly the Emperor. The usher told him that the Emperor was in the inner palace and took him and those of his village who remained across the courtyard and over a moat. The majordomo who opened the heavy door was truly resplendent, bedecked with ribbons. "This is finally the Emperor." They all knew this and bowed again, and he gave each a handful of silver coins. And many turned and left, marveling at their good fortune.

And so it went on as those who were left met ministers at various levels. Only the head man and one other were left when they met the grand vizier, and he gave each of them a magnificent diamond and bade them leave; and the last villager did.

But the head man was gently persistent and so the vizier opened the door to the throne room and there was the Emperor, who was dressed simply in white. And this time the head man knew that he was not mistaken and paid his respects with tears in his eyes. And the Emperor gave him much wealth and, more important, assigned him to his wise men for instruction so that he could one day assume a position in the royal court.

All of you are like the villagers who have set out on the journey. You will receive many benefits, like the copper and silver coins, as you do the exercises. Accept them gratefully, but do not think that they came from the Emperor. The Emperor has a much greater gift for you, and you will get it only if you are gently persistent.

It is my earnest hope that you will not stop until you have ignited a transformation process that will then take over by itself and carry you the rest of the way. That you do not turn back until you, too, have seen the Emperor. And once you have seen the Emperor, there is no turning back.

Good luck!

Mental models are pernicious creations and stoutly resist attempts to tamper with them. And yet, if you want quantum improvement in your life, you have to change many of your mental models and even replace some. This section introduces you to a select list of books that will move you in many different ways. They will pry open your mind and anchor you in the new foundation you are creating. An extended reading list appears in a later section.

Be open-minded as you go through these books. Most are quite easy to read but nevertheless profound. Some are tougher reading but still worth the effort. You may sometimes have to convert a frame of reference to another that makes more sense to you. Learning to do this is an important step in your own journey. Wisdom comes from many sources.

The books encompass many fields, including business, science, and spirituality. Read them at the rate of a book a month, and, if possible, form a book club that meets once a month to discuss the reading for that month. There are twelve books here, a full year's reading at the recommended rate.

Happy reading!!

1. Brunton, Paul, *A Search in Secret India,* Red Wheel/Weiser, 1990.
Paul Brunton was a journalist on a quest and visited many parts of the globe. The nature of his quest and the insistent questions that drove him may resonate with some of you. His observation is keen and his descriptions powerful. His matter-of-fact recital of some exceedingly strange experiences may leave some of you gasping. Suspend judgment and focus on the lessons he learned and would like to pass on. This book was written during the British Raj, and a colonial viewpoint does appear occasionally. Ignore this. This book is out of print. Order from www.cygnus-books.co.uk.

2. Senge, Peter M., *The Fifth Discipline: The Art and Practice of the Learning Organization,* Doubleday, 1990.
An MIT professor of organizational theory, Senge has also enjoyed a long tenure on best-seller lists and has coauthored two fieldbooks that show you how to turn your moribund organization into a learning one. He plugs a systems approach to solving problems so that today's solution does not become tomorrow's problem. Erudite and thoughtful, he has many important points to make, including the explicit recognition of how our mental models influence "reality" and the importance of gaining personal mastery. The writing is somewhat verbose, but stick with it.

3. Farson, Richard, *Management of the Absurd: Paradoxes in Leadership,* Simon & Schuster, 1996.
Psychologist, educator, and businessman, Farson has a penetrating insight into what is happening in today's business world. He illustrates his points with pithy sayings, such as, "The opposite of a profound truth is also true," "People we think need changing are pretty good the way they are," and "Organizations that need help most will benefit from it least." He is humorous but deadly serious and illustrates his points of view well.

4. Argyris, Chris, *Flawed Advice and the Management Trap,* Oxford University Press, 2000.
The subtitle of this book is *How Managers Can Know When They're Getting Good Advice and When They're Not,* and that is what the book is about. Argyris always has penetrating insight—if you have not read his other books, do so now—and he is superb at uncovering hidden agendas. He clearly demonstrates

the true feelings behind what is said and done and how the discrepancy affects organizational effectiveness. He also points out that there is more chaff than wheat in most consultant recommendations. The ideas are refreshingly new, but unfortunately the writing is labored, so reading is sometimes an effort.

5. DeMello, Anthony, *Awareness,* Image Books, Doubleday, 1990.
DeMello was a Catholic priest and a psychotherapist, and his retreats were legendary in their ability to inspire and transform the attendees. He died unexpectedly in 1987 and this book—edited by J. Francis Stroud, S.J.—is a compilation of his teachings and speeches. There are few books that are better at stripping away your egoistic defense mechanisms and forcing you to confront your true essence. If you truly ponder the implications of what he says, this book will shake your foundations.

6. Bohm, David, *Wholeness and the Implicate Order,* Ark Paperbacks, Boston, 1983.
A renowned physicist and collaborator of Einstein's, Bohm makes the point that scientists are too hung up on a fragmented worldview in which thought and matter are separate and distinct and the thinker is different from what he thinks about. He postulates that the Universe is an unbroken whole in which any element contains within itself the totality of the Universe. He also explicitly discusses consciousness, a subject most scientists shy away from. This book is sometimes a tough read.

7. Coelho, Paulo, *The Alchemist,* HarperCollins, 1993.
This is easy reading, but it is profound and has more layers than an onion. It is written like a parable—a form of exposition to which I am addicted—and talks about a shepherd boy who sets out to discover a great treasure and the strange personages who help him along the way. I hope that this book will inspire you to reach for your Personal Legend. You will understand when you read it.

8. Capra, Fritjof, *The Tao of Physics,* Shambala, 1975.
With the cult success of this book imitators swarmed in and there is now a "Tao" of everything from leadership to cooking. The author, a scientist in his own right, gives an overview of quantum physics and muses philosophically

on its implications. It is well written and you do not have to possess much of a scientific background to understand it. He is particularly good at drawing and explaining parallels between Eastern mysticism and modern physics. You may also wish to explore his coauthored book, *Belonging to the Universe.*

9. Hill, Napoleon, *Think and Grow Rich: The Original Version, Restored and Revised,* Aventine Press, 2004. (There are many publishers of this title; try to get this edition.)
Industrialist Andrew Carnegie, who may have been the world's richest man at the turn of the century, commissioned Hill to study the lives of the world's richest and most successful men and come up with a "success formula" that others could apply to their lives. He surveyed dozens of the top leaders of his time, including Theodore Roosevelt, John D. Rockefeller, Henry Ford, Alexander Graham Bell, Clarence Darrow, and Thomas A. Edison, and published his findings in a series of articles and papers. This particular volume has become a cult classic and is one of the all-time best sellers.

10. Greene, Brian, *The Fabric of the Cosmos: Space, Time, and the Texture of Reality,* Alfred A. Knopf, 2004.
A phenomenal book that gives you wonderful insights into modern science and specifically into quantum mechanics and astrophysics. He shows you how small anomalies in the real world have led to new theories that completely overthrow old scientific paradigms. This is a book that will make you gasp with awe at the power of the human mind and the wonder of the universe. Science, especially physics, has never been so enthralling.

11. Tolle, Eckhart, *The Power of Now,* New World Library, 1999.
The story goes that Tolle, at age twenty-nine, underwent a profound spiritual experience that destroyed his previous identity and plunged him into an inward journey that led to enlightenment. There are certainly many well-documented instances of something similar in spiritual literature, but don't waste your time trying to figure out if this is "true." Focus on whether what he says is helpful to your journey. He has much to offer, and the discussions of psychological time and the havoc it can wreak are profound. It has become a well-deserved best seller.

12. Dass, Ram, *Be Here Now,* Lama Foundation, 1971.

Formerly known as Richard Alpert, Ram Dass was a professor of psychology who was fired from Harvard because of his highly public experiments with psychedelic drugs. His subsequent peregrinations took him to India, where he found his Master and settled down to a drug-free spiritual practice. The first part of the book is a brief autobiography. The guy has a Ph.D. from Stanford and is well aware of the mental games we all play, particularly academics. The third part consists of plain-language essays on a variety of topics, such as money and the right livelihood, getting straight, the rational mind, etc. There are some great quotes in this section. The middle part is the kernel of the walnut—a series of cryptic statements about how life's odyssey really works, all richly illustrated with New Age graphics. This section will either make immediate and profound sense to you, or it won't. If it does, stick with it. If not, move on and don't worry about it.

SUPPLEMENTARY READING

The literature on creativity is vast. When you add to it the literature on how to figure out what you want to do and why, and sundry other topics, the available resources are mind-boggling. What follow are some of my highly personal and idiosyncratic recommendations. The books are organized in groups with a brief introduction to the group itself. Skim through many books in each of the groups. Read introductions, summaries, and tables of contents. Let your interests and inclination guide you. Follow your intuition. If you do not feel a sense of breathless excitement, drop the book and explore another.

I have—in most cases—given my rating of how the book reads. Reading level 1 is straightforward and easily understandable. Most gripping mystery thrillers and many trashy best sellers are written at this level. I have a strong preference for level 1 material because I firmly believe that if an author cannot communicate clearly then he/she probably has little worth saying. Reading level 3 is tangled and obscure and blessed by manufacturers of analgesics.

It includes language like "Item equivalence is a more concrete and microlevel perspective, and presupposes both construct and operationalization equivalence." Most academic "research"—including, alas, my own—is written at this level, and I invite you to share with me a moment of silence in memory of so many trees that have been so foully murdered. Reading level 2 falls squarely in between. It will not give you a headache, but neither is it a whiff of oxygen.

CREATIVITY

These are some other books on creativity that you might like. It is unlikely that you will learn new "techniques," but you may find a particular anecdote or mode of presentation to be powerful. Browse away.

Ackoff, Russell L., *The Art of Problem Solving,* John Wiley, 1978.
Wharton School professor and father figure in operations research Russ Ackoff is brilliant and incisive. He has an uncanny ability to frame problems so the solutions pop out, and he is funny to boot. There are many parables in the text, and these clarify some quite complicated analyses and lead to "morals," such as, "The less we understand something, the more variables we need to explain it."

———, *Management in Small Doses,* John Wiley, 1986.
Pretty much the same comments as above. Both books are at reading level 1.

Adams, James L., *Conceptual Blockbusting,* Addison-Wesley, 1987.
The author has a background as an engineer and Stanford professor. He defines various "blocks" to creativity, such as stereotyping, judging, etc., and suggests strategies to overcome them. The best parts are the exercises peppered throughout the various chapters. Be sure to try these. (Sample: Imagine the sensation of a long attack of hiccups.) Reading level 1.

DeBono, Edward, *Lateral Thinking,* Harper & Row, 1970.
Vertical thinking, according to DeBono, is digging the same hole deeper. Lateral thinking is digging someplace else. Junior is bothering his aunt, who is knitting a sweater. He feels constricted by the playpen and howls. Solution: Put the aunt in the playpen where she can knit undisturbed while Junior romps outside. Several sets of exercises are included. Reading level 1 with gusts of 2.

————, *Six Thinking Hats,* Little, Brown & Co., 1985.
DeBono describes hats of six colors, each associated with a different thinking mode. Putting on the white hat requires you to present facts and figures in a neutral, objective manner. The red hat requires you to present how you feel about "the proposal" emotionally, the black hat what your negative assessments are, and so on. The method is designed to switch thinking away from arguments into collaboration. Widely used techniques. Reading level 1.

————, *Serious Creativity,* HarperCollins, 1992.
Prolific as he is, it is easy to understand how DeBono can afford to live on his own private island. This book summarizes his other works and gives new anecdotes, business examples, and exercises. Reading level 1.

Isakson, Scott G., and Donald J. Treffinger, *Creative Problem Solving: The Basic Course,* Bearly Ltd., 1985.
This is a workbook that comes in a three-hole binder and provides detailed instructions on data finding, problem structuring, idea and solution finding, etc. The checklists of questions are quite helpful, though the text is somewhat boring. Reading level 1 but goes to 2 quite often.

Michalko, Michael, *Cracking Creativity,* Ten Speed Press, 2001.
The subtitle of this book is *The Secrets of Creative Genius,* and it is exactly that. The author is a creativity consultant with many Fortune 500 clients, and the business examples he gives are highly instructive. I particularly like the layout of the book and its excellent graphics. Use this as you would a recipe book, to search for ideas when you don't know what to cook. Pay particular attention to the strategies of thinking fluently and making novel combinations. Reading level 1.

Miller, William, *The Creative Edge,* Addison-Wesley, 1987.
A consultant to major corporations, Miller does a fine job of showing how to enhance creativity in individual and group settings. His discourse on intuitive methods is good, as is his discussion of human values. Methods of achieving "win-win" solutions in the workplace are neat. Reading level 1, very occasionally 2.

Parnes, Sidney J., *The Magic of Your Mind,* Creative Education Foundation, 1981. Another book that talks about the creative process, what blocks it, and how we can overcome the blocks. Many standard exercises are presented. The sans serif type is none too easy to read, but to compensate there is a profusion of cartoons, most of which are very, very funny. Reading level 1.

von Oech, Roger, *A Whack on the Side of the Head,* Warner, 1983.

————, *A Kick in the Seat of the Pants,* Harper & Row, 1986.
Nobody would publish his first book, so von Oech did it himself and created a blockbuster success that is still being touted by purveyors of manuals on self-publishing. It also established his reputation as a creativity consultant, and he picked up many prestigious Silicon Valley clients, including Apple Computers. Oversize and easy to read, this book has good graphics and pictures and fun exercises. Reading level 1.

The New Physics and Readings from Science

Quantum physics has turned topsy-turvy all of our cherished notions of how things work. In this world, time can flow backward, with particles dying before they are born. Space is curved and exists in an infinite number of dimensions. Space and matter are inexplicably linked; neither can exist without the other. The type of measuring instrument we use determines the nature of our observation; change one and the other changes as well. The act of observation alters that which is observed. A number of thinkers have raised the possibility that quantum phenomena have their counterparts in the "real" world, that too many of our assumptions are untested and probably false; and they have drawn strong parallels between the world views of Eastern philosophy and quantum mechanics. Be aware that others vociferously oppose the implications of such comparisons, and there are scientists of Nobel Prize–winning caliber on both sides of the argument. Leonard Shlain expresses it beautifully: "The new physics presently rests like a pea under the collective mattress of humankind, disturbing tranquil sleep just enough to begin to change how people think about the world." What is indisputable is that there are few exercises more capable of stretching your mind than pondering the status of Schrödinger's cat or the implications of the Einstein-Podolsky-Rosen experiment. Welcome to the mysterious world of physics!

And let us not forget other branches of science—pure mathematics, chemistry, biology and biochemistry, genetics, and many more. All these fields are in ferment, and the distinctions between functional areas are breaking down. Complex linear programming problems have been solved by DNA computers, leading to speculation that organic computers, vastly more powerful than their silicon-based counterparts, may soon be among us. Quantum computing is looming in the background. Even the merest exposure to what is happening "out there" in different fields will cause you to gape with wonder. Hold on to that feeling of awe, that amazement at where human thought has reached. You, too, will push the boundaries.

Casti, John L., *Paradigms Lost: Images of Man in the Mirror of Science,* William Morrow, 1989.
Casti, a mathematician by training, discusses deep questions, such as, "What is the true nature of mankind?" He considers quantum reality, extraterrestrial in-

telligence, and the origin of life. In each case he presents opposing viewpoints and the evidence for each and then puts on his judicial hat and plops on one side or the other. A particularly neat feature of this book is that Casti presents the social context in which many famous scientists worked and shows how their political and other beliefs contributed to their findings. Reading level 1, occasionally 2.

Dyson, Freeman, *Disturbing the Universe*, Harper & Row, 1979.
A physicist at the Institute for Advanced Studies at Princeton, Dyson worked with many of the most famous names in the field, including Oppenheimer and Feynman. The title of the book comes from a T. S. Eliot poem and serves to illustrate the breadth of the author's interests. He muses on many topics, from intergalactic colonization to nuclear and biological weapons, and has a keen feel for political reality. His description of the war years at Bomber Command in England is particularly worthwhile. Reading level 1 to 2.

Greene, Brian, *The Elegant Universe*, Vintage Books, 2000.
A marvelous exposition of the unexplained mysteries of physics with an especially lucid discussion of relativity. If Einstein's famous discovery still leaves you bemused, this book will give you understanding. The author is a strong proponent of string theory, and he explains how this may well be the theoretical underpinning for the much sought after "theory of everything." Reading level 1, very occasionally 2.

Gribbin, John, and Martin Rees, *Cosmic Coincidence: Dark Matter, Man, and Anthropic Cosmology*, Bantam, 1989.
A science writer and a physicist take you on an intriguing tour of some of the most revolutionary ideas to emerge from science: the particle zoo; black holes; cosmic strings; gravitational lenses; the Copenhagen and Many Worlds interpretation of quantum mechanics; and much more. Clear writing. Reading level 1 to 2.

Heisenberg, Werner, *Physics and Beyond*, Harper & Row, 1971.
The debate is raging again about whether Heisenberg, head of the Nazi equivalent of the Manhattan Project, was a courageous scientist who sabotaged the effort or an incompetent manager who fell on his face. There is no doubt that

he was one of the greatest physicists of all time, and his uncertainty principle is a cornerstone of our understanding of the universe. He muses on politics, history, religion, and other topics and reports on his conversations with other scientific greats like Einstein, Bohr, and Schrödinger. Reading level 2.

Jahn, Robert G., and Brenda J. Dunne, *Margins of Reality,* Harcourt Brace & Company, 1987.
A former dean of the School of Engineering at Princeton University and a NASA consultant, Jahn had a towering reputation that did not prevent vociferous attacks when he chose to investigate, using rigorous scientific methodology, subjects that were taboo then and are still largely so. The subtitle of the book is *The Role of Consciousness in the Physical World,* and he documents the results of his experiments showing that consciousness and matter interact in measurable ways. Reading level 2 with gusts of 3.

Morowitz, H., *Cosmic Joy and Local Pain: Musing of a Mystic Scientist,* Charles Scribner's Sons, 1987.
A Yale professor of biophysics muses on his field during a sabbatical and while on his sailboat in Hawaii. Many simple, and some quite complex, topics in science—the importance of water in organic life, energy flow, and entropy—are made clear in simple language. Reading level 1.

Newberg, Andrew, Eugene D'Aquill, and Vince Rause, *Why God Won't Go Away: Brain Science and the Biology of Belief,* Ballantine, 2001.
Mystics in many traditions speak of powerful experiences of unity, of merging with the universe, of becoming one with the cosmos. Most people dismiss such descriptions as metaphorical. But what if they are not? Modern science has provided us with ever more powerful tools to map the brain's neuronic activity. The authors report on studies that show that there is, indeed, such a state of merging and it is associated with a unique brain map. Neurotheology is a new discipline and it poses interesting questions, such as, "Did God create the Brain or did the Brain create God?" Reading level 1, sometimes 2.

Pagels, Heinz R., *The Cosmic Code: Quantum Physics as the Language of Nature,* Simon & Schuster, 1982.
Pagels, former president of the New York Academy of Sciences, does a pretty

good job of explaining how quantum physics evolved from Newtonian physics. He clearly explains the experimental anomalies of the latter, which forced the "creation" of the former. He also does an excellent job of describing the individual contributions of the great physicists who flourished in the 1920s and how the theoretical work of each tied in with that of others and cumulatively evolved into a fundamental shift in physics. Reading level 1, frequently 2.

Penrose, Roger, *The Road to Reality: A Complete Guide to the Laws of the Universe,* Alfred A. Knopf, 2004.
A great physicist and professor of mathematics at Oxford, Penrose provides a panoramic view of the evolution of physics and mathematics. He shows you the subtle interplays between the disciplines and puts historic rivalries between scientists into context. It encompasses everything from quantum particles to multiple universes. The author does make heavy use of mathematics and his language is not always lucid. The book is more than a thousand pages long. Much of it is reading level 3.

Schrödinger, E., *What Is Life? And Mind, and Matter?,* Cambridge University Press, 1969.
A Nobel Prize–winning physicist ponders on the implications of his discoveries: fate and free will; science and religion; the physical basis of consciousness; subject-object differentiation; and more. Reading level 2, sometimes 3.

Schwartz, Jeffrey M., and Sharon Begley, *The Mind and the Brain: Neuroplasticity and the Power of Mental Force,* HarperCollins, 2002.
The mind can shape the brain. What you intensely, deeply visualize can leave a permanent imprint on your brain. Many traditions say this, but until now you had to take it on faith. Now there is proof. Brain maps reveal that thinking does indeed create changes in brain waves. Also, the brain can rewire itself. The implications are profound and provide scientific rationale for the mental exercises propounded by religious teachers, sports coaches, and many, many others. Reading level 1.

Talbot, Michael, *Beyond the Quantum: God, Reality, Consciousness in the New Scientific Revolution,* Macmillan, 1986.
This is a well-written book that explains recent scientific experiments and why

they are important. True, he selects only experiments that further his point of view, but they are fascinating anyway. His thesis is that science will one day explain, or at least accept, mysticism and the paranormal and explores why so many scientists oppose them viscerally. Reading level 1 to 2.

Wilbur, K. (editor), *Quantum Questions: Mystical Writings of the World's Great Physicists,* New Science Library, 1984.
Collection of writings from a pantheon of Nobel Prize winners: Heisenberg, Schrödinger, Einstein, de Broglie, Pauli, Planck, and others. This book makes the case that, contrary to New Age thinking, contemporary physics does not "prove" mysticism. Nevertheless, every one of these giants was a mystic, and the book attempts to explore why. Fascinating reading as the towering figures of modern science reveal their personal beliefs and world views. Reading level varies from 1 to 3.

Zukav, Gary, *The Dancing Wu Li Masters,* William Morrow, 1979.
Wu Li is supposedly the Chinese word for physics. This is in the same tradition as Capra's *Tao of Physics* and is very readable. The discussions of philosophical quandaries—like whether Schrödinger's cat is alive and the implications of the Einstein-Podolsky-Rosen experiment—are well done. The last chapter, which deals with the limits of science, is fascinating. Reading level 1 to 2.

BUSINESS AND MANAGEMENT

The business world we live in is changing and the pace of this change is accelerating. The multilayered corporation with its autocratic hierarchy is unsuited to the new information era spawned by cheap computing power. People, and not machines or structures, are the key to an organization's long-run prosperity. Jack Welch, former chairman of General Electric, puts it as well as anyone: "The only way I see to get more productivity is by getting people involved and excited about their jobs. You can't afford to have anyone walk through a gate of a factory, or into an office, who's not giving 120%." His particular solution, which involves relentlessly raising the bar and subjecting employees to sometimes brutal treatment, may or may not be the best one, but it certainly has gained widespread attention and approbation. There are other companies that are also changing their organizational structures and processes to take account of the new reality. They are grappling with the problems of how, exactly, to empower workers and to get them to take ownership of problems. Consultants and academics are documenting the physical and psychic costs of continuing with the "old" ways. Just emerging is the recognition that there are physical and psychic costs of doing things in "new" ways. Herewith a small sampling of business and management books that you might find worthwhile. If you find any book particularly appealing, be sure to look up others by the same author. You will notice that I have an expansive notion of what constitutes a business or management book.

Albrecht, Karl, *The Only Thing That Matters,* HarperBusiness, 1992.
Albrecht has written or coauthored many books on customer service, and this is one of his better ones. The consumer seeks the best "value," not quality or low price. Albrecht explains how to ensure that you get and remain close to the customer. Illuminating anecdotes make points very clearly. Reading level 1.

Alexander, Col. John B., Maj. Richard Groller, and Janet Morris, *The Warrior's Edge,* Avon, 1990.
Alexander is a former Special Forces commander who led hundreds of search-and-destroy missions in Southeast Asia. He also studied meditation at Buddhist monasteries and helped bring visualization and mental techniques into the training programs of the U.S. armed forces. He is now a consultant to the army and a leading proponent of nondestructive warfare. The book teaches you how to get a mental edge and trust your intuition. Reading level 1.

Alsop, Ronald J., *The 18 Immutable Laws of Corporate Reputation,* Free Press, 2004.
Alsop is a veteran *Wall Street Journal* reporter who begins with the unarguable premise that an impeccable reputation is an invaluable corporate asset. He then talks about how to establish and sustain such a reputation. There is a lot of the usual stuff, such as great customer service, fixing problems right the first time, and so on. What makes this book valuable are the innumerable anecdotes that come from Alsop's day job. The examples make his points come alive and are useful guides to both what you should and should not do. Reading level 1.

Autry, James A., and Stephen Mitchell, *Real Power: Business Lessons from the Tao Te Ching,* Riverhead Books, 1998.
Autry was the CEO of the magazine division of the Meredith Corporation, which consisted of several powerhouses, such as *Ladies' Home Journal.* Since retiring, he has become a thoughtful exponent of the softer side of management, focusing on such themes as fulfillment, creation of a healthy work environment, and spiritual development. He writes simply on important topics, such as what is "control" and do you really need to do it. Good stuff, good quotes. Reading level 1.

Badaracco, Joseph L., Jr., *Defining Moments: When Managers Must Choose Between Right and Right,* Harvard Business School, 1997.
Ethical dilemmas in business do not always involve clearly right and wrong paths. They are frequently choices between principles that are both "right." A single mother with an ailing child is forced to leave work early on numerous occasions. Is it "right" to cut her some slack? Is it also "right" to fire her because her already overworked teammates are having to pick up that slack? Badaracco gives a framework in which to analyze such conflicts and talks you through its implications. Reading level 1.

Baker, Wayne E., *Networking Smart,* McGraw-Hill, 1994.
This is one of the better books on the subject of networking. Baker analyzes and categorizes the types of networks that exist in organizations and their usefulness in different situations, from providing support to members in trying times like downsizing to promoting teamwork and shared responsibility. He

also has excellent tips on how you fit into networks and how to create personal ones at your place of work. Reading level 1.

Bennis, Warren, *On Becoming a Leader,* Addison-Wesley, 1989.
A professor of management and a former university president, Bennis has written many books on leadership, and I am not sure that this is the best one. He asserts that leaders are made, not born, and that leadership cannot be taught; it has to be learned. He dissects the modern business environment and lists the essential qualities a leader has to have (integrity is one of them). Reading level 1 to 2.

Bianco, Anthony, *Rainmaker: The Saga of Jeff Beck, Wall Street's Mad Dog,* Random House, 1991.
Investment bankers, of course, have been known to stretch the facts. In fact, I am amazed that no "fairness opinion" has yet won an award for creative fiction. Even in this milieu, Jeff Beck stood out by fabricating everything from educational credentials to an exemplary, if totally fictional, war record. Bianco is a *BusinessWeek* writer who does a superb job chronicling Beck's rise and fall. The bigger value is in the peek this book gives into what life is really like in big prestigious banks. Dated but still accurate and very well written. Reading level 1.

Block, Peter, *Stewardship,* Berrett-Koehler, 1993.
Consultant and author Block espouses the notion of stewardship to replace the policing attitude of our institutions. He defines a patriarchy as an organization that is focused on control, consistency, and predictability. Responsibility for strategy lies with top management. He suggests partnership as an alternative in which there is the right to say "no," joint accountability, and absolute honesty. Interesting ideas. Reading level 2.

Byeham, William C., and Jeff Cox, *Zapp! The Lightning of Empowerment,* DDI Press, 1988.
A self-published book that became a million-copy best seller, this book helped propel Byeham's firm to great consulting success. Written as a fable, it talks of managerial behaviors that squelch initiatives (Sapp!) and how to change them so that workers feel empowered (Zapp!). Amusing and well

written but still has substance. A lot more difficult to do than it indicates. Reading level 1.

Byrne, John A., *Chainsaw: The Notorious Career of Al Dunlap in the Era of Profit at Any Price,* HarperBusiness, 1999.
A very well-researched look into Al Dunlap and his history of turning companies around. Most of the book focuses on Sunbeam—a public fiasco of the first magnitude—but the author also casts serious doubt on Dunlap's other "accomplishments." He points out, for example, that it was luck—and inept due diligence by Kimberly Clark—that prevented Scott Paper from being an equal failure. Many lawyers, accountants, consultants, investment bankers, and other service professionals conspired with Dunlap to keep his balloon from deflating due to complex factors ranging from greed to fear. The wonder is not that the debacle happened, but why it took so long to happen. There are no heroes in this book, and the author does an admirable job of probing the weakness of our business culture. Reading level 1.

Champy, James, *Reengineering Management,* HarperBusiness, 1995.
Half of the team that gave you *Reengineering the Corporation,* Champy took time off to ponder the consequences of what he helped unleash. This book is the result. It is a thoughtful examination of the "soft" side of business, of traits that managers must possess if their companies are to thrive as wholesome entities, not as cancerous growths. It encourages questions like "What kind of culture do we want?" and "What is this business for, anyway?" Lots of examples. Reading level 1.

Champy, James, and Nitin Nohria, *The Arc of Ambition,* Perseus Books, 2000.
Ambition can create prodigious achievement. The authors trace the accomplishments of a plethora of individuals, from Garibaldi to Jack Welch, and link their achievements to how a persistent vision would not let them be. They examine the roots of ambition and explain how you can use it to your advantage. They also caution against letting it wax into hubris—Al Dunlap is a classic, unbeloved example. Excellent examples from history, business, science, fiction, the military, and other sources. Reading level 1.

Chappell, Tom, *The Soul of a Business: Managing for Profit and the Common Good*, Bantam, 1993.

Chappell founded Tom's of Maine, built it into a thriving company, and then was wracked by questions like whether success in business automatically meant giving up personal values. He searched many places, including Harvard Divinity School. What is trust and how do you build it? How will workers handle autonomy, and how can you help them? Refreshingly candid discussions of how the author's views on such topics evolved. Reading level 1.

Charan, Ram, and Noel M. Tichy, *Every Business Is a Growth Business*, Times Business, 1998.

Two noted consultants and academics make the point that attitude and mindset, and not environment or circumstances, determine growth and success. They stress the importance of organizational continuity—does the "leader" have a succession plan in place?—and constant redefining of the market from the customer's perspective. Great anecdotes. Reading level 1.

Cialdini, Robert B., *Influence: Science and Practice*, Allyn and Bacon, 2001.

Cialdini is a psychologist, but he has written what may be one of the very best marketing books around. His research interest is how persuasion happens, how one person or entity can get another to do something that he/it wants. He has isolated six powerful principles by which this happens, and there is much variety in each. Many business examples and lots of pointers for further research. Reading level 1.

Cleary, Thomas, *Thunder in the Sky: On the Acquisition and Exercise of Power*, Shambala, 1993.

———, *Zen Lessons: The Art of Leadership*, Shambala, 1989.

Cleary, who holds a Harvard doctorate in East Asian languages, is best known for his translation of *The Art of War*, and has also translated dozens of other ancient Chinese works. Both of these books provide fascinating insights into leadership and the exercise of power from ancient practitioners well versed in the subject. Reading level 1.

Covey, Stephen R., *The 7 Habits of Highly Effective People*, Simon & Schuster, 1989.
This book was on paperback best-seller lists for more than three years. It makes very good points, such as "Every public victory is preceded by a private victory" and that you generally succeed when you "begin with the end in mind." Unfortunately, the language is labored and you have to plow through it. It would benefit greatly from the attention of a *Reader's Digest* book editor. Reading level 2.

Cowan, John, *The Common Table*, HarperBusiness, 1993.
Musings on life and work by a businessman, consultant, and parish priest. In the tradition of Robert Fulghum, as noted in the publisher's blurbs, but true nevertheless. There are personal anecdotes cleverly turned into lessons for corporations in a warm and nonpatronizing way. Take a small dose a day. Reading level 1.

————, *Small Decencies*, HarperBusiness, 1992.

Csikszentmihalyi, Mihaly, *FLOW: The Psychology of Optimal Experience*, Harper & Row, 1990.
FLOW is a state of intense absorption in which the distinction between you and the work you are doing practically disappears. Time appears distorted, with hours feeling like minutes or vice versa. Peak performers achieve this state regularly, and it has been extensively studied in champion athletes and sports figures as well as performers in the arts. University of Chicago psychologist Mihaly Csikszentmihalyi has researched the phenomenon in other occupations and explored the conditions under which FLOW can be achieved by practically anyone. Extraordinary creativity routinely occurs in the flow state. You may also wish to explore *The Evolving Self* by the same author. Reading level 1, occasionally 2.

DePree, Max, *Leadership Is an Art*, Dell, 1989.
The retired chairman of furniture maker Herman Miller, DePree has long been noted for innovative management practices. For example, he instituted a silver parachute for employees at his company so that they would be protected if they lost their jobs as a result of a hostile takeover. He outlines his philosophy of the covenant between a company and its workers. Most com-

panies are nowhere near it and not headed in that direction either. Reading level 1.

Feiner, Michael, *The Feiner Points of Leadership*, Warner Business Books, 2004. Feiner was the head human resources honcho at Pepsi-Cola and now teaches one of the most popular courses at Columbia Business School. He presents fifty "laws" of great leadership distilled from his observations over decades in the corporate world. Makes a strong case for integrity and remaining true to your values in the context of success in the executive suite. Reading level 1.

Goldsmith, Marshall, Beverly Kaye, and Ken Shelton, *Learning Journeys*, Davies-Black Publishing, Palo Alto, CA, 2000.
A bevy of best-selling authors, consultants, and trainers share personal stories about the event in their lives that was most significant and the lessons they learned from it. Warren Bennis, Stephen Covey, Jim Collins, and Goldsmith himself are some of the contributors. Some accounts are absolute gems and re-veal wisdom, compassion, and the way to growth. Reading level 1.

Hammer, Michael, *The Agenda*, Crown Business, 2001.
The sequel to *Reengineering the Corporation*, in which the author admits that it was no silver bullet. This time he talks a great deal about "process." You have to put systems in place that make it easy for a customer to do business with you and deliver overwhelming value. He also advocates breaking the boundaries between you, your suppliers, and your customers. Others—Jack Welch comes to mind—have said this earlier, but Hammer says it particularly well. Not quite as good in terms of showing exactly how to do what is prescribed. Still, it does make good points. Reading level 1.

Hammer, Michael, and James Champy, *Reengineering the Corporation*, Harper-Business, 1993.
Another longtime dweller on the best-seller lists that made the authors highly successful consultants. They advocate a fundamental redesign of work pro-cesses that will produce quantum leaps of productivity with an actual decline in resources used, and give several case studies. Unfortunately, "reengineering" has become a buzzword and a cloak for massive, frequently indiscriminate, layoffs. Reading level 1 to 2.

Handy, Charles, *The Hungry Spirit,* Broadway Books, 1998.
A British consultant with a blue-chip client list, Handy has a take on business that exposes its pompous self-contradictions. He muses on technology, the excesses of capitalism, and the growing evidence that markets do not always produce optimum allocations. His ruminations on the ethics of compromise and the purpose of profits are thought provoking. You might also wish to look up his other books, such as *The Age of Paradox.* Reading level 1.

Hanson, Marlys, and Merle Hanson, *Passion and Purpose: How to Identify and Shape the Powerful Patterns That Shape Your Work/Life,* Pathfinder Press, Alameda, CA, 2002.
Hanson's thesis is that we all have inherent motivational patterns that show up early in life and are dependably persistent. The trick to living a life of fulfilled potential is to understand our unique motivations and work so that they are used. The authors recommend a multistep process that involves identifying occurrences that gave you a sense of accomplishment from the earliest memories you have, analyzing them to detect patterns, and then reshaping your life to make use of what you have discovered. Reading level 1.

Harvey, Jerry, *The Abilene Paradox and Other Meditations on Reality,* Lexington Books, 1988.
Despite being a management professor, Jerry Harvey writes clearly and with wit. His essays examine the fundamental assumptions on which many management practices are based and find them faulty. He is particularly good at exposing hypocrisy and the euphemisms used to cover them up. Read the first essay and at least some of the others. *The Abilene Paradox* is also available on video, and you should watch it if you get a chance. Reading level 1.

Hawken, Paul, *Growing a Business,* Simon & Schuster, 1987.
Cofounder of the very successful mail-order gardening firm Smith & Hawken, the author has an unusual take on business. He emphasizes clearly that a successful business is an expression of a deep feeling welling up from the founder(s). This guiding principle is what shapes the business and makes it grow. Lucid discussions and some quite contrary assertions, such as money is secondary when starting a business. The author has since become a speaking celebrity. Reading level 1.

Heider, John, *The Tao of Leadership: Leadership Strategies for a New Age,* Bantam, 1986.

A clinical psychologist, Heider is a longtime student of the *Tao Te Ching* and has translated the spirit very well into modern management dilemmas. For example: "The wise leader knows that there are natural consequences for every act. The task is to shed light on these natural consequences, not to attack the behavior itself. If the leader tries to take the place of nature and act as judge and jury, the best you can expect is a crude imitation of a very subtle process. At the very least, the leader will discover that the instrument of justice cuts both ways. Punishing others is punishing work." Reading level 1.

Heifetz, Ronald A., and Marty Linsky, *Leadership on the Line: Staying Alive Through the Dangers of Leading,* Harvard Business School Press, 2002.

One of the better books on leadership. The authors, faculty members at Harvard's Kennedy School of Government, have many decades of experience with major companies, government agencies, and senior executives. They point out that true leaders do not find solutions as much as they create and hold the space in which others feel comfortable functioning and seeking and coming up with alternatives. With luck, one or more of these alternatives will work better than what is already in place. Reading level 1.

Johnston, David Cay, *Perfectly Legal,* Portfolio, Penguin Group, 2003.

The subtitle of this book is *The Covert Campaign to Rig Our Tax System to Benefit the Super Rich and Cheat Everybody Else.* That says it all. The author is a Pulitzer Prize–winning investigative journalist for the *New York Times* and makes extensive use of stories that he has filed. If you are poor, you pay taxes. If you are middle class, you pay more taxes. If you are wealthy, you hire a good tax attorney and pay proportionately much less. If you are super-rich, you frequently pay nothing at all. Not to the government, that is. You do pay the legion of accountants, attorneys, and financial advisors who dream up convoluted mechanisms to disguise income so that it does not have to be declared. Works for corporations and for individuals. Johnston explains in highly readable prose exactly how this is done. You will weep for our democracy. Reading level 1.

Komisar, Randy, with Kent Lineback, *The Monk and the Riddle,* Harvard Business School Press, 2000, 2001.

Software executive, angel, and iconoclastic thinker, Komisar is a firm proponent of the "big idea" that should permeate the very being of a company. This big idea springs from the values and vision of the founder(s), and Komisar stresses that the company should define its business in terms of where it is going and what it is becoming, not merely in terms of what it is. Written in the form of a fable in which a young would-be entrepreneur—Lenny—has an idea for a business to alleviate the pain of persons who have lost a loved one. In the pressure to raise funding for his venture, he jettisons the original idea in favor of what—in his opinion—will make a quicker profit. His partner finally takes steps that bring him back to the original idea, and this gets him the funding he needs. Reading level 1.

Langley, Monica, *Tearing Down the Walls: How Sandy Weill Fought His Way to the Top of the Financial Pyramid and Then Nearly Lost It All,* Free Press, 2002.

A wonderful account of how Sandy Weill rose, fell, and rose again, coming to almost J. P. Morgan–like prominence in the financial world. A really good glimpse into what happens in the world of high-level mergers and corporate governance, as well as how human foibles play themselves out in a larger arena. I cannot decide if Langley is being hagiographic or tongue-in-cheek when she describes Weill's characteristics. Gluttony, for example, becomes love of fine food and drink. Weill slashes benefits for employees while treating himself to top-of-the-line Gulfstream private jets. Would you want to be him? Reading level 1.

Lucht, John, *Rites of Passage at $100,000+,* Viceroy Press, 1997.

This book is a gem. Lucht is a headhunter, or, in polite parlance, an executive recruiter, and there is little about the business that he does not know. He shares this knowledge generously, with wit and passion. There is an excellent exposition on the similarities and differences between contingency and retainer recruiters. There are many, many useful tips on how, if unemployed, you can become speedily employed. He also provides revealing glimpses into the mores of large corporations. Reading level 1.

Mintzberg, Henry, *Managers Not MBAs,* Berrett-Koehler, 2004.
At last, someone who points out that the emperor has no clothes and, indeed, never had any. Mintzberg is a management professor at McGill University who makes the case that our business schools are churning out technically overqualified, cerebrally gifted, and morally deficient automatons who know nothing about how a business really works and also do not know that they know nothing. Others have made the same point, but Mintzberg is an "insider," so his data is stronger and his anecdotes more telling. Reading level 1.

O'Boyle, Thomas F., *At Any Cost: Jack Welch, General Electric and the Pursuit of Profit,* Vintage Books, Random House, 1998.
A former *Wall Street Journal* reporter chronicles the many ways in which GE under Jack Welch systematically used hard-nosed tactics to achieve its extraordinary stock market success. There is a seamy side to this success, including possibly illegal and certainly unethical corporate actions—verbal commitments disavowed, pension funds raided, customers given kickbacks, and competitive price collusion. GE wins court battles using overwhelming legal firepower, but the questions remain. Well written and well documented. GE pulled out all the stops to squelch this and largely succeeded. The points made about GE's culture are very relevant and have come to light in the wake of the company's declining share price and Welch's own well-publicized marital problems. Reading level 1.

O'Neil, John R., *The Paradox of Success,* Jeremy P. Tarcher/Putnam, 1993.
The subtitle of this book is *When Winning at Work Means Losing at Life.* A distinguished psychologist and consultant, O'Neil has run across more than his share of dysfunctional overachievers. He relates their tales along with analyses of why they became that way. There are descriptions of warning signs and suggestions to prevent you from traveling the same route. Serious issues treated sensitively. Reading level 1.

O'Shea, James, and Charles Madigan, *Dangerous Company,* Times Business, 1997.
The authors look at all of the major consulting firms and their individual legacies. There have been some spectacular success stories and quite a few fiascos, and the authors cover them all with engaging openness. Particularly useful is their insider's description of the culture of such major firms as Bain & Com-

pany, Boston Consulting, and McKinsey. Since these firms, between them, boast a majority of large companies as clients, you learn a great deal about how decisions are made at upper echelons. Reading level 1.

Owen, Harrison, *Riding the Tiger: Doing Business in a Transforming World,* Abbot Publishing, 1991.
A consultant who practices his trade on six continents, Owen pioneered Open Space Technology, a method of holding meetings that calls for little preparation and no preset agenda and is nevertheless fearsomely productive. An astute observer of the business scene, he has some penetrating comments on the change now wracking that scene. Like it or not, we are in this turmoil together and "he who rides the tiger does not always choose when to get off." Reading level 1 to 2.

Partnoy, Frank, *Infectious Greed: How Deceit and Risk Corrupted the Financial Markets,* Times Books, 2003.
The author is a law school professor with keen insight into how the evolution of trading instruments combined with human foibles and lack of regulation to give us spectacular fiascos, such as Long Term Capital Management, Enron, and WorldCom. If changes are not made now, much worse could follow. Reading level 2.

Pfeffer, Jeffrey, *The Human Equation: Building Profits by Putting People First,* Harvard Business School Press, 1998.
A Stanford Business School professor makes the case that financial success is best ensured by treating people as a valuable asset instead of merely paying lip service to the notion, as most companies do. Excellent case studies of such companies as SAS, which flourish by creating a nurturing environment for their workers. Reading level 1.

Ray, Michael, *The Highest Goal,* Berrett-Koehler, 2004.
The subtitle of this book is *The Secret That Sustains You Every Moment,* and it is very appropriate. The author states that each of us has a goal, one that can give every action and every moment of every day a deep meaning, and all of life is a quest to find this goal and work toward it. It is a powerful concept, and the author gives you methods to find your goal. Good exercises. Reading level 1.

Ray, Michael, and Rochelle Myers, *Creativity in Business,* Doubleday, 1986.
Ray is the Stanford Business School marketing professor who pioneered teaching creativity in a business school. The book contains many business anecdotes—now somewhat dated—and is very entertaining, but reading it like a novel will not do you much good. Practice the exercises he suggests, particularly those relating to the VOJ (Voice of Judgment) and those found in Chapters 4 and 6. Reading level 1.

Ray, Michael, and Alan Rinzler (eds.), *The New Paradigm of Business,* Jeremy P. Tarcher/Putnam, 1993.
Sponsored by the World Business Academy, an organization devoted to fostering responsible change in business, the book is a selection of articles and readings by businesspersons, consultants, academics, and journalists. The themes are cooperation, ethical responsibilities of business, and business as a vehicle for social transformation. Reading level 1 to 2.

Reichheld, Frederick F., *The Loyalty Effect,* Harvard Business School Press, 1996.
A Bain & Company consultant, Reichheld makes a persuasive case for loyalty-based management. He explicitly considers the lifetime value of customers and methods of increasing it. He extends the notion to employees, vendors, and other relevant stakeholders and even further to consider loyalty to values and principles. Excellent case studies. Reading level 1, very occasionally 2.

Rolfe, John, and Peter Troob, *Monkey Business: Swinging Through the Wall Street Jungle,* Warner Books, 2000.
Both authors are M.B.A.s from top schools who joined well-known investment banks in pursuit of fame and fortune. The scales fell from their eyes and they figured that a tell-all book could lead to the same outcome. Our financial powerhouses are not pretty places, and this book tells you why. Both authors have a good eye for the illustrative anecdote. Be warned that the language is sometimes risqué. Reading level 1.

Rosen, Robert H., and Paul Brown, *Leading People,* Viking, 1996.
The authors identify eight principles of leadership—such as vision, trust, creativity, and integrity—and give case studies of leaders, mostly group executives of companies with an occasional government or not-for-profit thrown in—

who are exemplars of each. Some of these cases are pretty good, but the few pages devoted to each preclude depth. You don't quite get to know how a company lauded for its creativity does on integrity. However, it does get you thinking. Reading level 1.

Schaffer, Robert H., *High-Impact Consulting: How Clients and Consultants Can Work Together to Achieve Extraordinary Results*, Jossey-Bass, 2002.
This is one extraordinarily worthwhile book, and I also liked its predecessor, *The Breakthrough Strategy*. The author's thesis is that most consulting projects fail because the consultant focuses on what needs to be done, almost never looking at what the client is able or willing to do. The correct way to proceed is to match what should be done with what the client can realistically do, given human and organizational constraints. Lots of tips and a strategy for how this can be done. It is written from the viewpoint of a consultant but is equally—or even more—useful for an executive trying to change things from the inside. Reading level 1.

Schwartz, Peter, and Blair Gibb, *When Good Companies Do Bad Things*, John Wiley, 1999.
Legions of well-known companies—Union Carbide, Shell, Nike, and Nestlé, for example—have been guilty of actions that have aroused broad public ire. Why do these ethical lapses occur, and is there any way of putting in place mechanisms to prevent them from happening? The authors take a remarkably balanced approach, neither castigating business as evil nor waxing rhapsodic over the benefits brought to Third World countries by their practices. They believe that the serious negotiations of the future will be between NGOs and multinational companies as the only two entities with truly global perspectives. Reading level 1 to 2.

Semler, Ricardo, *The Seven-Day Weekend: Changing the Way Work Works*, Portfolio, Penguin Group, 2004.
This is the guy who wrote *Maverick*, also a best seller. Semler runs a company in Brazil called Semco, which has sales of more than $200 million. It is also highly profitable and follows such totally unconventional practices as letting employees set their own working hours. Semler believes that in hypercompetitive markets the only way to win is to *give up* control to well-nurtured employees. He also believes that an important function of a company is to help

employees grow in diverse ways. When, oh when, will the rest of the world catch up with him? Reading level 1.

Senge, Peter, *The Dance of Change,* Doubleday, 1999.
Same coauthors as *The Fieldbook,* with George Roth as an addition. Same comments as for *The Fieldbook.* More recent examples of companies in the middle of change and more thoughts on the change management process. Reading level 1.

————, *The Fifth Discipline Fieldbook,* Doubleday, 1994.
This book, coauthored with Richard Ross, Bryan Smith, Charlotte Roberts, and Art Kleiner, tells you how to actually apply the theories propounded in *The Fifth Discipline.* It is simply written and chock-full of useful exercises, case histories, and practical tools. It is a thick tome, so take your time going through it and selecting what will be of most use to you. This is an excellent reference manual that lists great resources. Reading level 1.

————, *Presence: Human Purpose and the Field of the Future,* Society for Organizational Learning, 2004.
This book is coauthored with C. Otto Scharmer, Joseph Jaworski, and Betty Sue Flowers. The authors interviewed more than a hundred leading figures involved in organizational change and present a synthesis with many quotes. The focus is not just on how to make change happen, but on making sure that it is a nurturing change that benefits both the individual and the organization. Respect for the Universe is a strong subtext throughout. Reading level 1.

Sheth, Jagdish, and Andrew Sobel, *Clients for Life: How Great Professionals Develop Breakthrough Relationship.* Simon & Schuster, 2000.
The authors posit that the best consultants have ongoing—perhaps lifelong—relationships with clients and are consulted on a wide range of issues, even issues that are outside their expertise. Their advice is always valued and frequently heeded. Examples are Aristotle for Alexander, Cardinal Richelieu for King Louis XIII, Harry Hopkins for Franklin D. Roosevelt, and Thomas More for King Henry VIII. There are also more recent business examples. The advisor needs a special blend of empathy, depth of understanding, and integrity, and the authors define the qualities and how to develop them. Reading level 1.

Stewart, James B., *Disney War*, Simon & Schuster, 2005.
An excellent book about executive shenanigans at the company that Walt built. Painstakingly researched by a former *Wall Street Journal* reporter, the book makes you a fly on the wall in conference rooms where momentous decisions are made. The pettiness, greed, and sheer obtuseness of some of our corporate titans are laid bare with a scalpel. You will wonder how supposedly intelligent directors, charged with looking out for shareholder interests, ever permitted such antics. Reading level 1.

Stoll, Clifford, *Silicon Snake Oil*, Anchor Books, 1995.
The author is one of the pioneers of the Internet and plenty computer literate. He makes a searing case that computerization has gone too far and now detracts from the quality of life. He points out the many deficiencies of cyberspace and documents how the push to computerize schools is likely to produce even more illiterate and innumerate graduates than today's schools do, but at greatly increased cost. His arguments are compelling, but he pushes some of them a little too far. Judge for yourself. Reading level 1.

Sugarman, Joseph, *Advertising Secrets of the Written Word*, DelStar Books, 1998.

———, *Marketing Secrets of a Mail Order Maverick*, DelStar Books, 1998.

———, *Television Secrets for Marketing Success*, DelStar Books, 1998.
Joe Sugarman is the copywriting wizard who wrote incredibly entertaining full-page advertisements for high-technology gizmos. The company he founded, JS&A, was wildly successful and the precursor to others, such as The Sharper Image and DAK Industries. He is also the guy behind BluBlocker sunglasses. These books are a distillation of the marketing lessons he learned in a lifetime of entrepreneurship, and he is incredibly candid. He tells you what worked and why and what didn't work and why. Lots of real examples. Reading level 1.

Templeton, Sir John, *Discovering the Laws of Life*, Continuum Press, 1994.
Templeton is the mutual fund czar who founded the mutual fund family that bears his name and retained his honor while building an enormous fortune. Not an easy task. In this book he reveals the deeper principles by which he

steered his business career and invites you to do the same. They apply to your personal life as well. Do not be fooled by its simplicity and apparent naïveté— there is much wisdom here. Reading level 1.

Tichy, Noel M., with Eli Cohen, *The Leadership Engine*, HarperBusiness, 1997. Noel is a professor at the University of Michigan Business School and director of its Global Leadership Program. He takes you through the guts of many major organizations, such as General Electric and Ameritech, and dissects their culture. The chapter on values is particularly good, and the appendix—a handbook on how to create leaders in your turn—has much food for thought. Tichy's thing is that you should have your own "teachable point of view." I concur. Reading level 1.

Tichy, Noel M., and Stratford Sherman, *Control Your Destiny or Someone Else Will*, Doubleday, 1993.
Both authors are intimately familiar with General Electric and its charismatic leader, Jack Welch. They take you behind the scenes and show you what happened when Welch took over the reins from Reginald Jones, and why. They explain why one of America's biggest and most profitable companies was literally turned upside down and inside out, what the human cost of such turmoil was, and how the spectacular and well-documented productivity increases came about. You may like or abominate Welch, but it is indisputable that he set a trend in motion, and many, many companies are doing likewise with varying degrees of success. Read this book to find out what and why. Reading level 1 to 2.

Zander, Rosamund Stone, and Benjamin Zander, *The Art of Possibility*, Penguin Books, 2000.
Benjamin Zander is a conductor so passionate about music that he literally sways audiences into rapture. He is legendary for his preconcert lectures in which he educates his audience about the music about to be played. He also offers to refund the admission price of any member who is not emotionally moved. This is the kind of conviction that permeates this book. You, too, can be equally passionate about what you do. This book shows you how. Reading level 1.

Mind over Matter

There is an entire genre of books that basically postulates that you can create whatever you want by thinking about it. You can also change yourself, eradicating undesirable traits and inculcating positive ones. This genre is growing at an exponential pace, perhaps as a result of people's increasing frustration and inability to cope with the rapid changes taking place in the world today in all dimensions, from social mores to business practices. Many, but not all, of these books have a religious/spiritual underpinning and are deliberately inspirational. A few would lodge in the "self-help" section of giant bookstores. Do not look down your nose or scoff at them. I know chief executive officers of New York Stock Exchange companies who swear by some of these books and the exercises they suggest. You may well find something here that is highly relevant either in itself or as a springboard for further growth. Many of these books have been reprinted several times by different publishers. The publishers listed are either the original or very early editions.

Dyer, Wayne W., *Manifest Your Destiny: The Nine Spiritual Principles for Getting Everything You Want*, HarperCollins, 1997.
A popular speaker and author, Dyer has other books you may wish to explore, including *Real Magic* and *Wisdom of the Ages*. This book is a good manual on how you can use mental forces to create a physical reality. It contains good tips on how to harness the power of the subconscious mind, and the whole has an explicitly spiritual underpinning, which is quite common in this genre. Reading level 1.

———, *The Power of Intention: Learning to Co-create Your World Your Way*, Hay House, 2004.
This book is an excellent summary of all that the author has been saying for years, but the exposition is more lucid. He explains how each of us creates our

world through our inner dialogue and how we can change this dialogue to produce better results. Many chapters have a section at the end entitled Five Ideas for Implementing the Suggestions of This Chapter, which is valuable. Definitely one of his better books. Perhaps even his best. Reading level 1.

Fisher, Mark, *The Instant Millionaire,* New World Library, 1990.
This slim volume is written as a fable in which a young man seeks the secret of wealth from an elderly millionaire mentor. It discusses the power of focused thought, how to master your subconscious, and many similar topics in an easy, convincing style. The book contains many homilies, such as "Always remember that at a certain height there are no clouds. If there are clouds in your life, it's because your soul has not soared high enough. Many people make the mistake of fighting against their problems. What you must do is raise yourself above those problems once and for all. The heart of the rose will lead you above the clouds, where the sky is forever clear. Don't waste your time chasing the clouds, they will unceasingly reappear." Reading level 1.

Gawain, Shakti, *Creative Visualization,* Bantam, 1982.
An introduction and workbook for using mental energy to transform your life. There are many powerful affirmations and visualizations, along with tips on meditation. The startling success of this book catapulted the author to New Age cult status, and she promptly started giving workshops and lectures to large audiences. If you do explore this work, be sure to do the exercise on establishing your own sanctuary. Reading level 1.

Katie, Byron, *I Need Your Love—Is That True?,* Harmony Books, 2005.
Katie is one of the many authors who report having a sudden awakening experience that literally changed their lives. She was deeply unhappy before and wonderfully fulfilled after. Her first book—*Loving What Is*—was a best seller. In this book she focuses on relationships and points out that many of them become toxic because of the heavy demands we place on them to satisfy our own desperate needs. Reading level 1.

Maltz, Maxwell, *Psycho-cybernetics,* Prentice-Hall, 1960.
A plastic surgeon, Maltz was amazed at the psychological complications that were tied up with physical imperfections, whether real or imagined. He

found that his scalpel did not merely change a person's face; it changed a person's psyche as well and transformed many rundown hacks into spirited chargers. He elaborates on what you can do to take charge of your life, using well-tested psychological principles that make heavy use of autosuggestion. Reading level 1.

Peale, Norman Vincent, *The Power of Positive Thinking,* Prentice-Hall, 1952.
For half a century Peale was the beloved pastor of New York's Marble Collegiate Church and an inspiration to generations of his congregations. Still selling briskly after more than forty years, this book catapulted the author to preeminence as the confidant of presidents and the spiritual mentor of many movers and shakers. Simply and powerfully written, it calls for enlisting the help of Jesus Christ to solve a variety of human problems. Reading level 1.

Ponder, Catherine, *The Dynamic Laws of Prosperity,* Prentice-Hall, 1962.
Another book very much along the lines of *The Power of Positive Thinking.* In fact the author has been referred to as the "Norman Vincent Peale among lady ministers." It also talks about "prosperity laws" and how to apply them in your own life. Good sections on goal-setting and how to develop an attitude of abundance. Strong Christian religious undertone. Reading level 1.

Roman, Sanaya, and Duane Packer, *Creating Money,* H. J. Kramer, 1988.
This book was supposedly transmitted to the authors by a pair of "beings of light" who dwell in the higher dimensions. I have a problem with this, but that is my hang-up. It need not be yours. The book is simple to read, well written, and contains many exercises that absolutely work to help you achieve the stated goal of achieving wealth. There are two catches: (1) You must have an underlying worldview that is compatible with the exercises prescribed, and (2) The time frame can sometimes be a very long one. Read the introduction and the first three chapters. If you are not strongly attracted to it, drop the book. It will not work for you. Reading level 1.

Vitale, Joe, *Spiritual Marketing: A Proven 5-step Formula for Easily Creating Wealth from the Inside Out,* 1stBooks, 2002.
A slim, self-published volume, this book is shot through with typographical errors, grammatical excess, and sophomoric bromides. There are frequent refer-

ences to the author's friends, who are miracle workers, one and all. Despite its faults—and they are legion—the author makes some very good points on wealth consciousness and how to achieve it. You may well find benefit in his simple, sincere style. This book became an unheralded and underground best seller and was picked up by Amazon.com and other mainstream distributors. Reading level 1.

Wattles, Wallace D., *The Science of Getting Rich or Financial Success Through Creative Thought*, reprint, Iceni Books, 2002.
One of the early classics, this book is still highly relevant. First published in 1910, it is one of the clearest expositions of the Law of Wealth that I have come across. It is a powerful law and it works. And I will not say what it is, because the purpose of this introduction is to inspire you to get the book and find out for yourself. Reading level 1.

LIFE-CHANGING BOOKS

This is a loaded title for a section, and I have chosen it deliberately. What, exactly, is a life-changing book, anyway? If a precocious high school student reads a textbook on aerodynamics and, being inspired, subsequently becomes an aeronautical engineer, does that make it a life-changing book? If a young social misfit reads *Mein Kampf* and rises to head a supremacist group, does that make it a life-changing book? Whether the answer is yes or no depends on the perspective from which the question is asked. Life-changing books come in many flavors.

The books in this section are life-changing in the sense that they help you find answers to life's deeper questions: Why are we here at all? Where are we going? and so forth. This section will be particularly relevant to you if you have been gnawed by a question that won't go away: "Is this all there is to life?" There is a substratum to life on earth, a moral and spiritual bedrock as it were, that gives stability, direction, and purpose. You have to discover it on your own and learn how to use its power. Some of these books may help you on your journey of self-discovery.

The principal texts of the world's great religions, such as the Bible, the Bhagavad-Gita, the Koran, and the Dhammapada, are certainly sources of succor and strength. They have not been included here because they are already well known enough in their own right. The books listed, while they may spring from a particular tradition, have a broad appeal and a powerful message. Read many of them, but be warned that mere reading, even careful reading, is fruitless. You will only benefit if you "grok" them.

For those of you not familiar with Robert Heinlein's delightful work *Stranger in a Strange Land*, here is how one of the characters explains the term: " 'Grok' means to understand so thoroughly that the observer becomes part of the observed—to merge, blend, intermarry, lose identity in group experience. . . . If I chopped you up and made a stew, you and the stew, whatever was in it, would grok—and when I ate you, we would grok together and nothing would be lost and it would not matter which one of us did the eating." The concept itself is quite difficult to grok! Helpful hint: Do not rely too much on your analytical mind. The deeper, life-altering meaning is always revealed intuitively.

Be humble when you read any of these books, because there is deep wisdom there. If you find feelings of incredulity or disdain rising, stop immediately. There are two reasons for this: First, if such emotions arise, you will assuredly not be able to grasp what the book has to offer, so you might as well not waste any time. Second, at some later time in your life the message in that book may be precisely what you need. Why preclude yourself from such help by forming a negative impression now? Happy grokking!

No readability scores have been assigned to any of these books. They are generally simply written but have to be understood at many deep levels. Some books have been translated by more than one person and published by more than one firm. Some of these editions differ quite markedly from each other. Feel free to select the one that suits you best.

Al-Ghazali, Abu Hamid Muhammad, "al-Munqidh min ad-Dalal (Deliverance from Error)," in W. Montgomery Watt (tr.), *The Faith and Practice of Al-Ghazali,* Kazi Publications, Chicago, 1982.
Born in eleventh-century Persia, Al-Ghazali gave up a career as a distinguished academic to become a wandering ascetic. Widely acclaimed as the greatest Muslim after Muhammad, he makes a case for higher forms of human apprehension than the cognitive levels of normal functioning. He absorbed the philosophical texts and trod the way of the mystics. He presents his synthesis in simple language with deep conviction.

Augustine of Hippo, Saint, *Confessions,* tr. by R. S. Pine-Coffin, Penguin, 1961.
One of the early great leaders of Christianity, Augustine was a libertine deeply wedded to physical pleasure till his conversion at age thirty-two. This is a personal account of his search for truth, his wrestling with his libido and other passions, his repentance of his early ways, and the consecration of his life to Jesus.

de Mello, Anthony, *Contact with God,* Loyola University Press, 1991.
A Jesuit priest who passed away unexpectedly in 1987, de Mello achieved international renown for the workshops he conducted for both priests and laypersons. This book, which was published posthumously from his retreat notes, deals with how to use prayer as a powerful and effective means of bringing a spiritual presence into your life at all times; it also explains why you should strive to do this. You may also wish to explore *A Way to Love,* which is a series of meditations.

French, R. M., *The Way of the Pilgrim, The Pilgrim Continues His Way,* Ballantine, 1974.
Nobody knows who the Pilgrim was or much about his antecedents. Written in Russian, the manuscript was discovered years after his death and first published in 1884. The first English edition came in 1930. The Pilgrim was not

only unknown but also uneducated. He was crippled in one arm, dirt poor all his life, and frequently destitute. Yet his touching account of his unrelenting search for enlightenment has a raw power that has inspired countless others. And, despite his penurious outward circumstances, he found the "peace which passeth all understanding" by using a simple device. Read it to find out what and how, and try to do likewise.

Goldsmith, Joel, *The Art of Meditation,* George, Allen and Unwin, 1957.
A mystic himself, Goldsmith takes you by the hand and shows you how to meditate in simple, uncomplicated steps. Note that I said "simple," not "easy." Whether you find it easy or impossibly difficult depends on the strength of your intent. Goldsmith is unambiguous about the process, the experience, and the fruits.

Hahn, Thich Nhat, *The Miracle of Mindfulness,* Beacon Press, 1975.
A Vietnamese Zen master who now lives in exile in France, Thich Nhat Hahn has a writing style that is both gentle and insistent. He knows human foibles well, and his spirit of compassion is palpable. The book contains anecdotes and exercises designed to help you practice mindfulness, the Eastern skill of being awake and fully aware. As common in Buddhist traditions, breath is the vehicle used to bring you to mindfulness. The exercises will bring you relaxation, peace, and eventually self-awareness.

Ignatius of Loyola, Saint, *Spiritual Exercises,* tr. by Thomas Corbishley, P. J. Kennedy & Sons, 1963.
A Spanish nobleman, Ignatius of Loyola left court life to enter the army. Recovering from severe wounds suffered at the battle of Pamplona, he read several books by and about the early saints and underwent a remarkable conversion that led to his hanging up his sword at the Benedictine monastery of Montserrat. He entered the priesthood, founded the Jesuit order, and was its first superior-general. While practicing austerities and meditation, he underwent mystical experiences that formed the basis for this book. These are powerful contemplative exercises.

Lawrence, Brother, *The Practice of the Presence of God,* H. R. Allenson, London.
Nicholas Herman of Lorraine, a footman and soldier, uneducated and lowborn, entered a Carmelite monastery in seventeenth-century France. By the time he died at age eighty, he was known as Brother Lawrence and deeply revered for his saintliness. The latter trait shows through in this book, particularly in the spiritual maxims and gathered thoughts. Practical, devotional, and inspirational.

Maimonides, Moses, *The Guide for the Perplexed,* tr. by M. Freidlander, Dover, 1956.
Born in Córdoba in the twelfth century, Maimonides became a physician at the court of Saladin as well as one of the most influential philosophers of his day. The guide reconciles scriptural texts with the findings of the science of its time. There are lucid expositions of topics such as the impossibility of ascribing any positive attributes to God. While this is quite worthwhile, it is heavy reading.

Nikhilananda, Swami, *The Gospel of Sri Ramakrishna,* Ramakrishna-Vivekananda Center, NY, 1942.
Ramakrishna was the untutored nineteenth-century mystic and sage who proclaimed, through personal experience, that the endpoints of the world's major religions were identical. The best Western account of his life and times is Christopher Isherwood's *Ramakrishna and His Disciples.* This book is a translation of a Bengali work that recounts details of his conversations with his disciples and visitors. Much of Ramakrishna's teachings were transmitted through parables.

Osborne, Arthur, ed., *The Teachings of Sri Ramana Maharshi,* Rider & Co., London, 1962.
Ramana Maharshi was the Indian saint introduced to the West by Paul Brunton in *Search in Secret India.* An exponent of the philosophical system of Advaita Vedanta, he espoused the short, direct solution to the human predicament: self-inquiry. Steady and continuous investigation into the nature of the mind transforms the mind and resolves it into its source. Read *Ramana Maharshi and the Path of Self-Knowledge* by the same author first. If that makes a deep intuitive appeal to you, follow up with this book.

Palmer, G. E. H., Philip Sherrard, and Kallistos Ware, tr. and ed., *Philokalia*, Faber and Faber, 5 vols.
These are the writings of the early church fathers compiled by St. Nikodimos of the Holy Mountain and St. Makarios of Corinth, men of deep spirituality who found simple, powerful ways to bring the presence of God into everyday life. Springing as they do from personal experience, their writings are deeply moving. The *Philokalia* was the only book the Pilgrim carried apart from the Bible.

Teresa of Ávila, Saint, *Autobiography*, tr. and ed. by E. Allison Peers, Image Books, Doubleday, 1959.
Teresa of Ávila was in her late teens when she entered a Carmelite convent in Spain in 1533. A series of visions helped her find her life's work helping to reform the Carmelite order and bring it back to austere ways and its spiritual roots. The book is a moving description of her trials and tribulations, early doubts, and how she always found strength when she needed it most.

Thomas à Kempis, *The Imitation of Christ*, tr. by Betty I. Knott, Fontana, 1963.
Relatively little is known about Thomas à Kempis, a German-born Dutch religious of the fourteenth century. Even the attribution of this work to him has been contested. It is a powerful and simple interpretation of the teachings of Jesus and the attitude needed to benefit from them in daily life. Immensely practical, it does not dwell on theological points. It goes instantly to the heart of man's predicament: how to gain happiness and freedom from suffering by learning the truth.

PARADIGM BUSTERS

Thomas Kuhn is the person who popularized the notion of a paradigm: an internally consistent framework in which we function, whether in science, medicine, politics, or any other field. Out-of-the-box thinking, the kind that produces truly revolutionary solutions to intractable problems, is simply the breaking of these powerful mental models. Sometimes, very rarely, the unsuitability of a particular paradigm is realized in an instant. Recollect the scene in the movie *Gandhi* when communal tensions were running high and bereaved victims were set to engage in retaliatory violence. Gandhi's quiet admonition "An eye for an eye makes the whole world blind" effected an instant transformation. In the West, notions of justice are inextricably linked with retribution. The truth councils of South Africa turned this concept on its head and helped large numbers of people, of all races, come to terms with the horrific occurrences of the recent past. It was an imperfect and incomplete process, but it too represents a paradigm shift. This section lists several books that defy conventional thinking in mainstream circles. Some of them have excellent ideas that have perhaps been extrapolated too far. Others have not gone far enough. Many of the books in other categories, particularly Life-Changing Books and The New Physics, are also paradigm busters.

Abraham, Jay, *Getting Everything You Can out of All You've Got: 21 Ways You Can Out-Think, Out-Perform and Out-Earn the Competition,* St. Martin's Press, 2000. Jay Abraham is a marketing genius. This genius is not as well recognized as it deserves to be. In part this is because he loudly and frequently proclaims his expertise and is thus discounted by the discriminating. He has incredibly profound and useful marketing insights and has published them in many reports that are not commercially available. See a sample of his stuff at www.abraham.com. He also has a finely nuanced understanding of how spiritual principles affect wealth and how it is built. This book is not the best he has to offer, but it is still well worth your while, especially the last chapter. Reading level 1.

Gallwey, Timothy W., *The Inner Game of Tennis,* Bantam Books, 1974.
There is the tennis that you play on the court. And then there is the tennis you play in your head. The latter is much more important and greatly influences the former. Contains excellent tips on how to break out of bad habits effortlessly in strokes of all kinds by substituting new good habits. The same techniques work as well in life. This is a classic, and it is easy to understand why it became a best seller. Reading level 1.

Jaworski, Joseph, *Synchronicity: The Inner Path of Leadership,* Berrett-Koehler, 1996.
Jaworski is a successful lawyer from a distinguished family in the profession—his father was the Watergate special prosecutor. This book is a chronicle of the son's journey from hard-charging, high-living attorney to thoughtful exponent of the principles of relationships and interconnectedness. He gives interesting accounts of how he came to realize that we create the world in which we live and how there is an underlying unity in the Universe, which embraces animate and inanimate matter. Reading level 1.

Kauffman, Stuart, *At Home in the Universe,* Oxford University Press, 1995.
A MacArthur Fellow and a Santa Fe Institute professor, Kauffman is a renaissance scientist, flitting easily between physics, biology, and the history of science. He makes a powerful case that evolution by natural selection, the essence of Darwinism, is only a part of reality. Complex entities, from megalopolises to megacorporations, "self-organize" according to rules of complexity theory that are only beginning to be understood. If this is true, there is profound hope for solving many of humankind's most intractable problems. In any event, the book is fascinating reading. Reading level 2.

Kennedy, Dan, *The Ultimate Success Secret,* Kimble and Kennedy Publishing, Austin, TX, 1999.
This is a slim, self-published book. The binding is poor, the pages aslant, the font varies from page to page, and the general production is of very poor quality. There are also typos galore, grammatical mistakes, and virtually every other fault you can find in a book. Despite this, the book is a gem. The author has had little formal education but has both keen observation and penetrating insight. He bootstrapped his way to financial success and has an impeccable reputation as a marketing wizard. This book is part how-to and part personal philosophy, and well worth your while. Reading level 1.

Kohn, Alfie, *Punished by Rewards,* Houghton-Mifflin, 1993.
Our entire society is based on the concept of rewards and incentives. Teachers hand out stickers to kindergartners. Human resources vice presidents agonize over merit pay raises. Best sellers advise managers to catch employees doing something right and then praise them. Kohn argues that this is a fundamen-

tally flawed approach, because punishment and reward are two sides of the same coin. In his view, rewards rupture relationships, discourage risk-taking, and actually reduce intrinsic motivation. He also propounds alternatives. Lots of footnotes and references. Reading level 1, frequently 2.

Korten, David C., *When Corporations Rule the World,* Berrett-Koehler, 1995. We operate under the assumption that liberal democracy, as we understand it, is the "best" form of government and the prescription to salvation for Third World countries as well as the many countries released by the fall of the communist USSR. Korten, a former Harvard Business School professor, asserts that the market system spawned by this form of government is actually responsible for much of what ails humanity. Institutions such as the World Bank and the International Monetary Fund are captives of the system and perpetuate it to the detriment of entire countries and peoples. Corporate colonialism has replaced the other kind and is greatly exacerbating inequality of all kinds. Many footnotes and references. Reading level 1.

Lakoff, George, *Don't Think of an Elephant!,* Chelsea Green Publishing, 2004. Be warned that Lakoff is highly partisan and his Republican bashing could greatly irritate supporters of that U.S. political party. He is a professor of linguistics and illustrates, in a wonderfully lucid way, how the language in which we describe a problem shapes our views of it. Though he never uses the term, this is a book about mental models—how they are formed and how they can be foisted on a gullible public by shrewd manipulators. Entertaining and revelatory. Reading level 1.

Morehouse, David, *Psychic Warrior,* St. Martin's Press, 1996. In the Cold War era the CIA funded a top-secret psychic espionage program. Morehouse was one of the small number of trained psychics who were part of that program, and he recounts his tales of the rigorous training and double-blind tests of validity. His story is that he broke philosophically with the CIA because something as miraculous as remote viewing was a gift to humankind and he did not like it being used solely as an espionage tool. Facing court-martial for improper disclosure of classified material, he was discharged from the army and generally harassed. Researchers at other institutions, such as the Princeton Engineering Anomalies Laboratory, have independently corroborated much of what he says—in terms of results obtainable. Morehouse's account is self-serving in some ways, and you might want to look up Jim Schnabel's *Remote Viewers* for a journalist's perspective of the same events. Reading level 1.

Phillips, Michael, *The Seven Laws of Money,* Shambala, 1993.
Phillips has had a checkered career in and out of corporate life. He was a bank executive and one of the persons who helped set up what is now MasterCard. In this book he takes a hard, candid look at some of our dilemmas regarding money and also posits some unusual rules that govern the money in our lives. See if you can relate to this: "The treadmill is a common example. People work hard to provide themselves and their families with worldly goods, new and better toys, better appliances. It's something we joke about so often—keeping up with the Joneses. Yet the process of working for more money so consumes our time and is considered so valid by our peers that we never stop to consider our values, our priorities." If this strikes a chord, read the book. Reading level 1.

Robbins, John, *The Food Revolution: How Your Diet Can Help Save Your Life and Our World,* Conari Press, 2001.
The author is the son of the cofounder of Baskin-Robbins and thus heir to one of the great American fortunes. The book is a searing indictment of factory farming as well as the treatment of animals generally. Factual and fact-based, the book makes the case that our food industry, especially the meat-poultry part of it, is destructive to your health and well-being. Throw in the moral dimension as well and the boat is truly foundering. He also lays out economic and environmental reasons for a change in our diet away from animals as food. Compelling presentation. Reading level 1.

Shroder, Tom, *Old Souls: The Scientific Evidence for Past Lives,* Simon & Schuster, 1999.
Shroder, a *Washington Post* journalist, reports on the work of Dr. Ian Stevenson, professor at the University of Virginia, who has documented more than two thousand cases of reincarnation. Quite a skeptic when he began, Shroder traipsed behind the good doctor in remote parts of the world and personally witnessed his research procedures and fieldwork. He found the evidence overwhelming, and there were cases on many continents. Now he too echoes Dr. Stevenson's refrain, "Why?" Why will the scientific community still not accept

such findings? Why is there reluctance to even study the subject more closely, given the immense amount of groundwork that has already been done? Scientists have open minds, right? Or do they? Reading level 1.

Singer, Peter, *Writings on an Ethical Life,* HarperCollins, 2000.
A collection of essays from many of his previous works, this book will make you think. Singer is the poster child for animal rights as he decries "speciesism," the unthinking assumption that human life is more sacred than any other. He also has unconventional views on abortion, poverty and how to alleviate it, and a host of similar topics. When Princeton offered him a professorship, wealthy donors like Steve Forbes threatened to withhold support. He certainly arouses strong feelings. His logic is unassailable, and he bases his arguments on clearly articulated assumptions. Reading level 1.

Thought Provokers

These are books that pose questions and provide solutions that can have very deep meaning. Quite possibly, some of these belong in the Life-Changing or Paradigm Buster categories. In any case, they will force you to confront the inner life that most of us tend to shy away from contemplating.

Allen, James, *As a Man Thinketh,* Grosset & Dunlap, 1980.
It will take you less than an hour to go through this slim volume, but it may well take a lifetime to implement the simple methods he suggests and reap their full harvest. *The Path to Prosperity* and *The Way of Peace,* companion volumes, are equally good. This book shows you how the inner world that you create with your thoughts eventually manifests as the outer world that you experience. Reading level 1.

Barian, Mark, *The Roar of the Ganges,* Eshwar, India, 1999. Available from the bookstore at www.arshabodha.com.
Barian was a successful computer entrepreneur with a big house and all the trappings of the American Dream. He became a monk in a classic Indian tradition with a lifelong vow of poverty. This book recounts how this transformation occurred, but it is much more than that. It is also a lucid explanation of concepts such as the true nature of happiness and how it can be achieved. Barian has a wry sense of humor and makes his points with pithy stories. This book is a real gem.

Boldt, Laurence G., *Zen and the Art of Making a Living,* Arkana, 1993.
The subtitle of this book is *A Practical Guide to Creative Career Design,* and it is that and more. The best book, by far, that I have come across on how to identify what your strengths are, how to visualize your ideal job, and how to go about bringing it into existence. Hundreds of inspiring quotes and dozens of thoughtful checklists. If you go through this book with care, it will assuredly be life changing in addition to thought provoking. Reading level 1.

Bornstein, David, *How to Change the World,* Oxford University Press, 2004.
This is a book about social entrepreneurs and, in particular, about Bill Drayton and Ashoka. In the Ashoka model, a rigorous screening process identifies persons who have come up with innovative solutions to some pressing social problem. Overwhelmingly, these persons arise from those who are deeply and personally affected by the problem. If the solutions are scalable and the social entrepreneur exceeds high bars for personal dedication and ethical behavior, he becomes an Ashoka Fellow and receives a three-year stipend that frees him from earning a living while he further develops his idea. More than a thousand Ashoka Fellows of both sexes are quietly improving the lot of millions of persons around the world. Reading level 1.

Fleischman, Paul R., *Cultivating Inner Peace,* Jeremy P. Tarcher/Putnam, 1997.
The author tries to deliver on the title by defining "inner peace" and outlining simple steps that can be taken to reach the state where the noise and violence is all outside you. He makes reference to powerful role models, such as John Muir, Walt Whitman, Gandhi, Thoreau, and Tagore, and draws lessons from their privations and methods of dealing with them. Reading level 1.

Fox, Matthew, *The Reinvention of Work,* HarperSanFrancisco, 1994.
A defrocked Dominican priest, Fox is a cult figure in his own right. He has written a thoughtful treatise on the meaning of work as opposed to jobs. Here is a quote: "Jobs are to work as leaves are to a tree. If a tree is ailing, the leaves will fall. Fiddling with leaves is not going to cure an ailing tree; just as one cures an ailing tree by treating its roots, so we cure the crisis in work by treating the root meaning and purpose of work." Drawing on the experience of mystics from all parts of the globe and tying it to a modern framework, Fox offers an alternative vision of the definition of work, the compensation of work, and its infusion with ritual and healing. Reading level 1.

Frankl, Victor E., *Man's Search for Meaning,* Pocket Books, 1984.
There are many editions of this book. Just pick one that is revised and updated. Frankl lost most of his family in Nazi concentration camps and wondered why, under such horrific conditions, some persons blossomed beyond belief while others sank into a morass of depression and self-pity. Deeply compassionate, he recognizes that guards, too, could be victims and details the risks some took to be kind to their charges. How many concentration camp inmates would be capable of saying "It is apparent that the mere knowledge that a man was either a camp guard or a prisoner tells us almost nothing. Human kindness can be found in all groups, even those which as a whole it would be easy to condemn." And what is it that gives meaning to life? Read the book to find out. Reading level 1.

Kabat-Zinn, Jon, *Wherever You Go, There You Are,* Hyperion, 1994.
A beautiful title, and the statement is indisputable. Kabat-Zinn, who is a stress-reduction specialist with the University of Massachusetts Medical Center, talks about action, patience, simplicity, trust, generosity, and similar topics. Chapters are brief and there are exercises at the end of many. Reading level 1.

Kapleau, Philip, *Zen: Dawn in the West,* Anchor Books/Doubleday, 1980.
Founder of the famous Zen center at Rochester, Roshi Kapleau made Zen accessible to Americans by stripping away the cultural outgrowths while retaining the essence. This book contains discourses, dialogues, answers to questions, letters, and commentaries on texts. He gives practical instructions on such matters as what unwholesome thoughts are and how one should get

rid of them. His earlier book, *The Three Pillars of Zen,* is a classic and also worth perusing. Reading level 1.

Kornfeld, Jack, *A Path with Heart,* Bantam, 1993.
Trained as a psychologist, Kornfeld has a deep appreciation of the human predicament. He talks about spiritual practice, the difficulties inherent in the path, and methods of coping with them. The language is simple and the meditation exercises quite powerful. Good explanations of such phenomena as the "dark night" mentioned by St. John and descriptions of altered states. Reading level 1.

Krishnamurti, J., *Think on These Things,* Harper & Row, 1964.
An excellent compilation from public talks given by Krishnamurti in many settings. He fields questions on ambition, attention, simplicity of life, self-discipline, and like topics. He is penetratingly lucid and rather sharp at times but always unconventional. His goal is to break you out of mental stupor, and his discourses on the nature of mind and thinking do a fine job of this. Reading level 1.

Lavenia, George, *What You Think Is What You Get: Realizing Your Creative Power and True Potential,* Earth Foundation, 1997.
Another of those books that tell you that you create your world and everything in it. That you are responsible for anything in your life that is not working well and can change it at will. What makes this book different is the simplicity of exposition, the power of the examples, and the quotes, sayings, and meditations. Savor it like a fine wine and spend hours following each train of thought it opens up. It will be time well spent. Reading level 1.

Needleman, Jacob, *Money and the Meaning of Life,* Doubleday Currency, 1991.
Money is the great taboo in our society. We scramble after it and animatedly discuss what ballplayers, celebrities, and chief executives make. We do not ever discuss what money means to us, what compromises we make in life in our own quest for it, and how big a place it occupies in our thinking and actions. Needleman, a philosophy professor, discusses such topics as the limits of material happiness and whether money can buy love. This book will help you accept and come to terms with money in your own life. Reading level 1.

Sennet, Richard, *The Corrosion of Character,* W. W. Norton, 1998.
This is a series of essays and reports on interviews with bakers, barmaids, and advertising executives. There are ruminations on the nature of work and time in our new postindustrial economy and how the advantage of flexibility may perhaps be more than overshadowed by the loss of a sense of purpose. Many questions, few answers, but then the author does not believe that there are any easy answers. Reading level 1.

Shore, Bill, *The Cathedral Within,* Random House, 1999.
A social entrepreneur himself, Shore talks about the need to give back, to do something that benefits society, to find meaning in one's life. Great cathedrals, such as the one in Milan, survive for centuries. This is because "Somehow, it had been both communicated and understood that it wasn't just that building a truly great cathedral would require everyone to share their strength, but rather that everyone sharing their strength would result in a truly great cathedral." Many stories of remarkable individuals who have inspired such effort and a great list of others. Reading level 1.

Thurman, Robert, *Inner Revolution,* Riverhead Books, 1998.
A onetime Buddhist monk, personally ordained by the Dalai Lama, Thurman is now a professor at Columbia University and a mini-celebrity in his own right. He has done as much as anyone to focus attention on the plight of Tibet and the atrocities it has been subjected to. In this book he argues that the "cool revolution" launched by the Buddha, as opposed to revolutions that involve violence and bloodshed, is a model worth emulating and a phenomenon that is still far from having run its course. He tellingly makes the point that military prowess cannot be equated with greater civilization and presents an alternate vision of how governments and citizens can relate to each other. Reading level 1.

Ullman, Robert, and Judyth Reichenberg-Ullman, *Moments of Enlightenment,* MJF Books, Fine Communications, NY, 2001.
This book was previously published as *Mystics, Masters, Saints and Sages.* Enlightenment is a goal in many traditions, and many are the travelers who have arrived there. Each serves as a unique beacon that appeals to still others. This book is a collection of the enlightenment experiences of several Masters, rang-

ing from the supremely well known, such as the Buddha, St. John of the Cross, and Ramana Maharshi, to the relatively unknown, such as Suzanne Segal and A. H. Almaas. In most cases the accounts are in their own words and the cultural contexts come across clearly. Reading level 1.

Walsch, Neale Donald, *Conversations with God: Book 1,* Putnam, 1996.
This book purports to be a conversation with the Big Cheese—the author poses the questions and transcribes answers, which appear automatically. It was on the *New York Times* best-seller list for nigh on two years. Despite these two strikes against it, it has profound insights into the nature of human suffering, life, and liberation. A particularly good explanation of how thought leads to manifestation. Reading level 1.

RESOURCES

———➤•◄———

I think of this book as a beginning, the start of a quest of self-exploration and fulfillment that will last the rest of your life.

I hope you feel the same way and would be glad of company on this journey of a thousand miles. You have merely taken the first step and there are many thrills of discovery in front of you.

You are invited to join the community of like-minded travelers. Please visit:

www.areyoureadytosucceed.com

You will find a plethora of resources, including new exercises, readings, and recommended books, newsletters, Web sites, audio-visual suggestions, news about talks and other events, and much, much more. You will always find much to help you on your journey, and you will get support when you find yourself flagging.

HIGHLY RECOMMENDED MAGAZINES

Ode is a magazine that comes out ten times a year. Each issue has many articles that give you a different take on some aspect of our complex existence. It is reaffirmative of the human spirit and can be very uplifting. See **www.odemagazine.com** for details. Do subscribe.

Worthwhile comes out six times a year and is devoted to "Work with Purpose, Passion, and Profit." It profiles businesses that contribute to the larger society and people who have unusual ideas about how businesses should be organized. Each issue will leave you with a greater sense of possibility. See **www.worthwhilemag.com** for details. Again, do subscribe.

Science of Mind is a pocket-sized monthly magazine. It has Christian roots but does not hesitate to print articles by the Dalai Lama and leaders of other traditions. It was founded by Ernest Holmes, who is extensively quoted in each issue. There are many uplifting, one-page ruminations entitled "Daily Guides" in each issue. See **www.scienceofmind.com** for details.

MISCELLANEOUS

Visit **www.globalideasbank.org** for creative ideas to solve many personal and social problems.

The site **www.MarshallGoldsmithLibrary.com** has many excellent articles and other material.

ACKNOWLEDGMENTS

Many people helped, in different ways, to make this book appear in reality. Some are not even aware of their contribution. I can only acknowledge a few, and I do this gratefully and humbly. Thank you from the bottom of my heart.

Swami Chinmayananda, whose talks on Sankara's *Mohamudgara* in New York in 1975 were a turning point in my life.

Swami Dayananda Saraswati, for his electrifying exposition of Vedanta in camps at Bard College, New York, and Cedar Crest College, Pennsylvania, in the late seventies.

My father, who encouraged me to read and made sure that I was always well supplied with books, and my brother Nagendra, who, at one stage, introduced me to many books that became life-long friends.

Janet Falk, who was the first to recognize the power inherent in the course and encouraged me to keep at it . . . and her late husband, Arnold, who threw open their house to all seekers who visited.

Lisa Queen, who is still my agent but has moved to good friend and trusted advisor.

Mrs. K. S. Varalakshmi, my mother-in-law, who provided loving care to my father and freed time for me by doing so.

Michael Ray, whose course at Stanford Business School was an inspiration and who was always gracious in his help.

Dr. Jeffrey Trilling, our family physician, who intuitively understands the principles in this book and brings them into his medical practice.

The guest speakers who gave so generously of their time and contributed so greatly to the success of the course: Andy Krieger, Marshall Goldsmith, Mort Meyerson, Alex von Bidder, Frances Hesselbein, N. R. Narayana Murthy, Rajat Gupta, David Brown, Robert Thurman, Bill Drayton, Malcolm Gladwell, Gretchen Morgenson, Robert Knowling, Stever Robbins, Jim Kuhn, and others.

Sho Albert, Sreedhar Kona, and Brandon Peele, who helped with the course and the book in ways too numerous to mention.

Emiliya Zhivotovskiy, whose creative bugging kept me on schedule; Sandra Navalli, who created the book list on Amazon.com and manages the alumni invitations; and Rafael Mier, for facilitating the retreats.

My teaching assistants, who put so much of themselves into each session: Josh Klenoff, Alan Iny, Alexandra Marchosky, Nicole Archer, Durre Nabi, Paulo Lima, Geoff Carleton, Katherine Calderwood, Rebecca York, Anu Oza, Jason Blake, and others.

Joan Digby, who encouraged me to develop the course and offered it repeatedly in the Honors program of Long Island University.

Walter Beebe, who made constructive suggestions when I was creating the syllabus and offered the program at the New York Open Center.

Peter Boyd, Ove Haxthausen, Suzanne Aptman, and Christian Bluemel, who worked together to offer the program through the Columbia Business School Alumni Club, New York.

Liz Perle, who smoothed the text and made it so much more readable.

Tony Adzinikolov, who created a compelling promotional DVD for the course.

Shirish Joshi, who felt drawn to the course and undertook creation of the Web site as a labor of love.

The administrators at Columbia Business School, who saw the impact the course was having and extended their support: Paul Glasserman, Safwan Masri, Kathleen Swan, and Nayla Bahri.

Paddy Barwise, Julia Tyler, and Ruth Allen, who brought the course to London Business School, and Magnus Asbjornsson, who persuaded dozens to sign up for it with help from Pranav Nahar and Ishani Chattopadhyay.

The wonderful folks at Hyperion, who strongly supported the book at all stages—it would not have happened without their support: Will Schwalbe, Bill Strachan, Ellen Archer, Katie Wainwright, Jane Comins, Christine Ragasa, and Jessica Wiener.

And last, but by no means least, the many, many students who had the courage to take such an unconventional course and the greater courage to embark on a lifelong journey of self-discovery. I learned so much from them collectively. There is no space to list all their names, but I am forever grateful and indebted to them.